STAR TREK SPEAKS

Also by Susan Sackett:
LETTERS TO STAR TREK

*THE MAKING OF STAR TREK—
THE MOTION PICTURE*
(co-author with Gene Roddenberry)

Also by Stan Goldstein and Fred Goldstein:
STAR TREK SPACEFLIGHT CHRONOLOGY

Also by Fred Goldstein:
THE TV GUIDE QUIZ BOOK

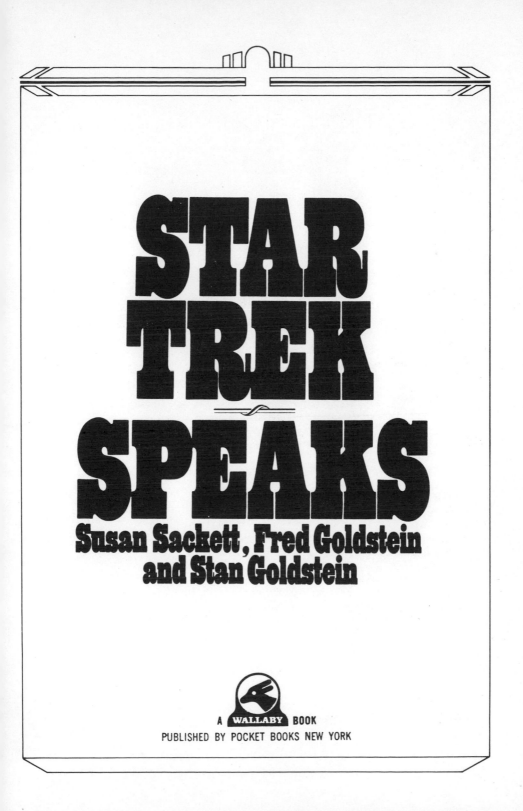

STAR TREK SPEAKS

Susan Sackett, Fred Goldstein and Stan Goldstein

A WALLABY BOOK

PUBLISHED BY POCKET BOOKS NEW YORK

POCKET BOOKS, a Simon & Schuster division of
GULF & WESTERN CORPORATION
1230 Avenue of the Americas, New York, N.Y. 10020

ISBN: 0-671-79091-9

First Wallaby printing October, 1979

10 9 8 7 6 5 4 3 2 1

Printed in the U.S.A.

CONTENTS

SUSAN SACKETT
To Mac and Gert,
for letting the Black Sheep have the last baa.

FRED GOLDSTEIN
To Phyllis,
for her understanding and confidence on the long journey.

STAN GOLDSTEIN
For the people who believe in tomorrow.

"To all mankind—may we never find space so vast, planets so cold, heart and mind so empty that we cannot fill them with love and warmth."

—Star Trek, "Dagger of the Mind"

INTRODUCTION

By the late 1960's America was a nation of television addicts. No longer content with grays, blacks and whites, we rejoiced when sophisticated electronics and miniaturization at last brought the price of color television sets within the reach of the majority of American families. As sales of these sets soared, the three major networks made the switch to all-color, although the selection of color programs being offered was still very limited. Most viewers escaped the realities of the 60's (the Vietnam war, protests and riots, assassinations and political upheaval) through the medium of television, welcoming such light-weight fare as "Gomer Pyle," "Gilligan's Island," "Petticoat Junction," "Green Acres," "The Flying Nun" and "The Beverly Hillbillies."

September 8, 1966, saw the debut of a television program of a different color. It was called "Star Trek," and it too was in glorious rainbow hues. However, the program went a step beyond the usual escapism. In the course of seventy-nine original one-hour dramas, "Star Trek" spoke about aspects of life, death, humanity, society and a host of other universally understood concepts in a way seldom seen before on television. Indeed, its phenomenal success and loyal following is directly attributable to its unyielding optimistic outlook for the human race. The U.S.S. *Enterprise* is viewed by millions as our ambassador to the rest of the galaxy. Her crew is the embodiment of all the good we, as a race, can be, exhibiting the right combination of strengths and weaknesses that allow for the true human spirit to be evident to all.

The brainchild of Gene Roddenberry—a former pilot and policeman-turned-writer/producer/philosopher—"Star Trek" captured an audience which was, to a degree, in the forefront of a great change that swept the land. From the anti-war movement to the civil rights movement to the ecology movement, young-thinking people everywhere were expressing their opinions and deeply felt sentiments about the sorry state of our country.

But because television, a medium that exists to sell sponsors' products, had given the censor more power than the creator, Gene Roddenberry couldn't be as up-front about our collective problems as the demonstrating millions were. If he wanted to say something important and meaningful about the mess we were in, he would have to do it another way. And what better forum than an action-adventure series which appeared to be nothing more than good drama. Roddenberry felt he couldn't be accused of rocking the boat with a twenty-third century starship; strange-looking aliens on far-off worlds with their problems and struggles made good entertainment, but certainly no parallels could be drawn between purple, polka-dotted people and ourselves! The network censors never did catch on.

But "Star Trek," like any prophet, was without honor in its own time and place. The NBC network cancelled the *Enterprise's* five-year mission after only three years had elapsed (1966-1969). It may have had several million loyal viewers—enough support to achieve a million-letter campaign to save the series for a second and third season—but there were not enough millions to appease the great god Neilsen, and the *Enterprise* plummeted to the depths of rerun syndication.

It was not until the 70's, when "Star Trek" appeared in over 140 domestic and fifty foreign markets, that an overwhelming awareness of the series occurred. "Star Trek" garnered high ratings in reruns, attracting a wide range of admirers of all ages, from all walks of life, resulting in a cult-like phenomenon that is still on the rise. Books, records, merchandise, conventions, fan clubs, publications and a multi-million dollar "Star Trek" motion picture have only partially quenched the incredible thirst for more "Star Trek."

This book is a natural by-product of the growing awareness of the importance of "Star Trek" in our culture today. It is a compilation of the ideas and ideals, the wisdom and commentaries which "Star Trek" originally expressed weekly. Many of these quotes, which are really dialogue spoken by various "Star Trek" characters, will be familiar to "Trekophiles," those adoring fans of the program who are able to quote whole passages of dialogue verbatim. Other remarks, more obscurely buried in the scripts of various episodes, were culled by our own laborious scrutiny of each final draft script. You may perhaps recall these lines only after another rerun viewing. (Check this week's episodes!)

As we began to compile the material we wished to quote in this book, we gradually became aware of certain natural categories. The eleven chapters of Star Trek Speaks! represent the major topics commented on by the program: the problems of everyday life; humans and their frailties, as well as their achievements; ideals of love and the joys of life in general; the tragedy of waste and destruction, and so on. In setting up the chapters, the three of us attempted to place the quotations in a logical order under topics which seemed appropriate. More often than not, we ended up arguing amongst ourselves on the proper pigeonholing of each quote. Should this one go under "Universal Truth," or is it an expression of feeling and more appropriately classified under "Emotion and Logic?" After working many long hours we settled upon the present setup. We don't expect total agreement from each reader, as there is bound to be a good deal of overlapping of categories. And certainly every thought that was ever given in "Star Trek" will not be covered here, but we feel that every main idea expressed in the series has been represented.

Eventually, after reading a selection of quotations, one begins to see a fairly consistent philosophy. The behind-the-scenes force for this unity and consistency was "Star Trek's" creator, Gene Roddenberry. Each week, through the input he supplied to such noted writers as Harlan Ellison, Ted Sturgeon and D. C. Fontana, Roddenberry was able to use "Star Trek" effectively, as a means of expression for his personal philosophy. Sometimes he was serious and dealt with war, racial prejudices and death; other times he allowed his childlike wonder and awe of things about him to creep into a weekly episode, marveling at the universe, or poking fun at the human creature. It is because of this aspect of "Star Trek"—its dramatization of people the way they really are—that the program has remained powerful and relevant, its timeless thoughts speaking perhaps more loudly and clearly today than ever before.

Susan Sackett,
Fred Goldstein,
Stan Goldstein,

March, 1979

CHAPTER ONE

UNIVERSAL TRUTHS

"Star Trek" addressed itself to the full spectrum of the universe. No matter on what distant planet or in what remote area of the galaxy the *Enterprise* crew may have found themselves, certain truths were held to be constant, unbounded by time and space. If something were true for one life form, then it ought to be so for all, on a galactic scale. Such things as basic as freedom, truth, the nature of time and eternity, moral precepts, and our relationships to these concepts were all dealt with in the course of weekly episodes.

One highly stressed ideal is the universal concept of freedom: freedom of expression and development to full potential for all life forms; freedom to acquire knowledge, which should be available to all who wish it. Indeed, freedom itself is mandated by unlimited mental development. The mind must be given free reign in the universe regardless of the consequences, but if the acquisition of knowledge and the mind's expansion get out of hand, we are also warned that this evolutionary step may have its pitfalls.

In order for there to be universal freedom, beings must be devoid of prejudices in relationship to each other. In these "one on one" situations, "Star Trek" speaks to the individual, and more specifically, addresses itself to the *soul* of the individual—perhaps hinting at a belief in the immortality of the soul. What is good for the development of the individual soul? What should be the laws of the individual in overall relationship to the laws of the universe or "God?"

Concurrent with this development on the individual level is the society's need for a morality awareness, the prime moral conviction being the sanctity of life, which must be guaranteed to all. The taking of life, causing harm, pain or suffering to others is contrary to universal moral laws, and often we find that the eternal conflict of good and evil may be the underlying theme of an entire episode.

"All your people must learn before you can reach for the stars."

Kirk, "The Gamesters of Triskelion,"
stardate 3259.2.
The Thrall Shana has asked Kirk to
take her with him to the stars.

"We have found all life forms in the galaxy are capable of superior development."

Kirk, "The Gamesters of Triskelion,"
stardate 3211.7.
Kirk does not feel that the Providers
have achieved this state.

"Knowledge, sir, should be free to all!"

Harry Mudd, "I, Mudd,"
stardate 4513.3.
Mudd has not payed royalties to the
owners of patents he sold. He defends
his position in a light-hearted way.

16

"The more complex the mind, the greater the need for the simplicity of play."

Kirk, "Shore Leave,"
stardate 3025.8.
The Caretaker's race, highly
advanced by Earth standards, created
the planet's amusement facilities
for their own recreation.

"When a child is taught . . . it's programmed with simple instructions—and at some point, if its mind develops properly, it exceeds the sum of what it was taught, thinks independently."

Dr. Robert Daystrom, "The Ultimate Computer,"
stardate 4731.3.
Daystrom thinks of his M-5 computer
as a child, learning and growing.

"No problem is insoluble."

Dr. Janet Wallace, "The Deadly Years,"
stardate 3479.4.
Janet's optimistic reply to Kirk
that they will come up with a solution
to the unknown affliction.

"Genius doesn't work on an assembly line basis. You can't simply say, 'Today I will be brilliant.'"

Kirk, "The Ultimate Computer,"
stardate 4731.3.
McCoy wants to know why the M-1
through M-4 computers were not
entirely successful if Dr. Robert
Daystrom is such a brilliant man.

Dr. Richard Daystrom—
THE ULTIMATE COMPUTER

"Superior ability breeds superior ambition."

Spock, "Space Seed,"
stardate 3141.9.
The "supermen" bred by Earth's initial
eugenics program were overly aggressive
and arrogant.

*"There comes to all races an ultimate crisis which
you have yet to face. . . . One day our minds became
so powerful we dared think of ourselves as gods."*

Sargon, "Return to Tomorrow,"
stardate 4768.3.
Sargon cautions Kirk that we are yet
too primitive to have faced the ultimate
crisis.

*"It's hard to believe that something which is neither
seen nor felt can do so much harm."*
*"That's true. But an idea can't be seen or felt. And
that's what kept the Troglytes in the mines all these
centuries. A mistaken idea."*

Vanna the Troglyte and Kirk, "The Cloud Minders,"
stardate 5819.0.
Vanna finds it hard to believe
that the zienite emits a gas which,
although invisible, retards the
mind and heightens the emotions.

"Insufficient facts always invite danger."

Spock, "Space Seed,"
stardate 3141.9.
Spock suspects there may be some
danger from the sleeper ship.

"History tends to exaggerate."

Colonel Green, "The Savage Curtain,"
stardate 5906.4.
Colonel Green defends himself when
Kirk questions how history has
portrayed him.

*"Even historians fail to learn from history—they
repeat the same mistakes."*

John Gill, "Patterns of Force,"
stardate 2534.7.
Gill realizes the non-interference
directive is the only way for space-
farers.

"... freedom ... is a worship word ... "
"It is our worship word too."

Cloud William and Kirk, "The Omega Glory,"
stardate unknown.
Kirk's mention of the word "freedom" has sparked
a response from the previously silent
Cloud William. Kirk agrees, hoping to
gain his trust.

*"... the prejudices people feel about each other
disappear when they get to know each other."*

Kirk, "Elaan of Troyius,"
stardate 4372.5.
Elaan, the Dohlman, despises Troyians,
yet is committed to marry one.

"There's a way out of any cage."

Captain Christopher Pike, "The
Menagerie" ("The Cage"),
stardate unknown.
Imprisoned by the Keepers, Pike
expresses the human need for freedom.

"Most legends have their basis in facts."

Kirk, "And The Children Shall Lead,"
stardate 5029.5.
Spock has told Kirk of the planetary
legend that the evil was awaiting a
catalyst to set it into motion.

Captain Christopher Pike—
THE MENAGERIE

"Many myths are based on truth."

Spock, "The Way to Eden,"
stardate 5832.3.
Kirk asks Spock if the passengers really
believe that the planet Eden exists.

"Is truth not truth for all?"

Natira, the High Priestess of Yonada,
"For the World is Hollow and I Have
Touched the Sky,"
stardate 5476.4.
The Oracle tells Natira that the
stranger's truth is not her truth.

Natira, the High Priestess of Yonada—
FOR THE WORLD IS HOLLOW AND I HAVE
TOUCHED THE SKY

"There is an order of things in this universe."

Apollo, "Who Mourns for Adonais?"
stardate 3468.1.
Apollo tells Carolyn Palamas he will
provide mankind with its every need.

"Time is fluid ... like a river with currents, eddies, backwash."

Spock, "The City on the Edge of Forever,"
stardate 3134.0.
Spock is responding to Kirk's question
of where McCoy will arrive in the past.
The currents that swept McCoy into a
certain time and place might sweep them
to the same place.

"Without freedom of choice there is no creativity. Without creativity there is no life."

Kirk, "The Return of the Archons,"
stardate 3157.4.
Kirk realizes he must logically outwit
Landru (the machine) in order to release
the people of Beta 3 from its control.

"Change is the essential process of all existence."

Spock, "Let That Be Your Last Battlefield,"
stardate 5730.2.
Spock believes that perhaps Lokai
of Cheron can change his prejudiced
attitude.

"A little suffering is good for the soul."

Kirk, "The Corbomite Maneuver,"
stardate 1514.0.
Kirk's reply to McCoy, who is defending
the crew's diminished proficiency due
to tiredness.

*"If there are self-made purgatories, then we all have
to live in them."*

Spock, "This Side of Paradise,"
stardate 3417.7.
Spock explains to Leila why he must
live the Vulcan life style he has
chosen for himself.

"Killing is stupid; useless!"

McCoy, "A Private Little War,"
stardate 4211.8.
McCoy comments to Kirk that Tyree, the
leader of Neural's hill tribe, has the
same beliefs we do.

"We have the right to survive!"
"Not by killing others."

Deela, the Queen of the Scalosians and
Kirk, "Wink of An Eye,"
stardate 5710.5.
Deela plans to perpetuate her own
species in a manner which will prove
fatal to the *Enterprise* crew members.

"Murder is contrary to the laws of man and God."

M-5 Computer, "The Ultimate Computer,"
stardate 4731.3.
Kirk is attempting to trap the M-5 computer in a round of
logic regarding its programming.

"Prepare for tomorrow—get ready."

Edith Keeler, "The City On the Edge of Forever,"
stardate unknown.
Edith has summarized her optimism and
faith in the future with these few words.

Leila Kalomi, Mr. Spock—
THIS SIDE OF PARADISE

"Killing is wrong."

Losira the Kalandan, "That Which Survives,"
stardate unknown.
Kirk asks the strange woman how she
feels about trying to kill him.

*"Madness has no purpose. Or reason. But it may
have a goal."*

Spock, "The Alternative Factor,"
stardate 3088.7.
Spock comments on Lazurus' purpose in pursuing his
adversary.

*"Punishment becomes ineffective after a certain
point. Men become insensitive."*

Eneg of Ekos, "Patterns of Force,"
stardate 2534.7.
Eneg admonishes his subordinate about
the use of physical punishment to obtain information.

*"No one may kill a man. Not for any purpose. It
cannot be condoned."*

Kirk, "Spock's Brain,"
stardate 5431.6.
Kara the Eymorg believes that taking
Spock's life is justified because it
will serve the need of her people.

*"Where there's no emotion, there's no motive for
violence."*

Spock, "Dagger of the Mind,"
stardate 2715.1.
Vulcan society's answer to hostility.

"Uncontrolled, power will turn even saints into savages. And we can all be counted on to live down to our lowest impulses."

Parmen, the Platonian leader, "Plato's Stepchildren,"
stardate 5784.3.
Parmen realizes that were it not
for the controls of the Federation,
the Platonians would revert to their
power abuses.

"Violence in reality is quite different from theory."

Spock, "The Cloud Minders,"
stardate 5818.4.
Spock hopes the Cloud Dwellers will
reconsider using violence in subjugating
the Troglyte miners.

"If a man had a child who'd gone anti-social, killed perhaps, he'd still tend to protect that child."

McCoy, "The Ultimate Computer,"
stardate 4731.3.
McCoy thinks that Dr. Robert Daystrom
feels fatherly protection towards
his M-5 computer.

"A father doesn't destroy his children."

Lt. Carolyn Palamas, "Who Mourns for Adonais?"
stardate 3468.1.
Kirk and the landing party have angered
the god Apollo. Lt. Palamas, concerned
for their safety, appeals to Apollo's
parental instincts.

"After a time, you may find that having *is not so pleasing a thing, after all, as* wanting. *It is not logical, but it is often true."*

Spock, "Amok Time,"
stardate 3372.7.
Spock admonishes Stonn, who now has
possession of T'Pring.

"Youth doesn't excuse everything."

Dr. Janice Lester (in Kirk's body), "Turnabout Intruder,"
stardate 5928.5.
Janice Lester is still bitter, after
all these years, that Kirk walked out
on her.

"Without followers, evil cannot spread."

Spock, "And The Children Shall Lead,"
stardate 5029.5.
The children are being used by the evil force, and Spock
realizes the threat they present to
the *Enterprise.*

"Evil does seek to maintain power by suppressing the truth."
"Or by misleading the innocent."

Spock and McCoy, "And The Children Shall Lead,"
stardate 5029.5.
Spock and McCoy speculate on what could have
destroyed the people on the planet, and
suspect an unknown entity may be using
the children for an evil purpose.

"It would seem that evil retreats when forcibly confronted."

Yarnek of Excalbia, "The Savage Curtain,"
stardate 5906.5.
Yarnek comments when Kirk succeeds in getting the representatives of evil to retreat.

"Yes, it is written. Good shall always destroy evil."

Sirah the Yang, "The Omega Glory,"
stardate unknown.
Kirk attempts to convince both the
Yangs and the Kohms to go back to their
original political knowledge and study
the old documents. There is much to be
gained by applying them to the present.

"Sometimes a man'll tell his bartender things he'll never tell his doctor."

Dr. Phillip Boyce, "The Menagerie" ("The Cage"),
stardate unknown.
Boyce, anxious to help Christopher Pike reveal
his troubles, has just handed Pike a
martini.

"Beauty is transitory."
"Beauty survives."

Spock and Kirk, "That Which Survives,"
stardate unknown.
McCoy says that Losira the Kalandan must have been a
beautiful woman. Spock comments, and
Kirk disagrees with him.

"Another dream that failed. There's nothing sadder."

Kirk, "This Side of Paradise,"
stardate 3417.3.
Kirk comments on the possible demise
of Omicron Ceti III colony.

Dr. Leonard McCoy, Captain Kirk, Mr. Spock—
THIS SIDE OF PARADISE

"We're all sorry for the other guy when he loses his job to a machine. But when it comes to your job—that's different. And it always will be different."

McCoy, "The Ultimate Computer,"
stardate 4729.4.
McCoy knows Kirk is worried about being replaced by
a computer.

"Not one hundred percent efficient, of course . . . but nothing ever is."

Kirk, "Metamorphosis,"
stardate 3219.8.
The "universal translator" is, like
all things, not perfect.

"No one can guarantee the actions of another."

Spock, "Day of the Dove,"
stardate unknown.
Spock says that Mara cannot speak for her husband, Kang, the
Klingon Commander, even in the
dangerous situation which all of them
are experiencing.

"Every living thing wants to survive."

Spock, "The Ultimate Computer,"
stardate 4731.3.
Spock indicates that Dr. Richard
Daystrom probably impressed the
instinctive reaction for survival on
the M-5 computer.

"It is necessary to have purpose."

Alice, android #1, "I, Mudd,"
stardate 4513.3.
Harry Mudd gave the robots an objective
after the last of their makers had died.

"Virtue is a relative term."

Spock, "Friday's Child,"
stardate 3499.1.
McCoy has used all the elements of
psychiatry he knows, yet Eleen still
doesn't want her baby, much to his
dismay.

"There are always alternatives."

Spock, "The Galileo Seven,"
stardate 2822.3.
Scott wonders what alternatives
there could be, since they have no fuel.

CHAPTER TWO

VULCANS AND ALIENS

Although most of this book's commentaries are expressed by, or about human beings, we decided to include a chapter about Vulcans and other aliens for several reasons. It is often easier to be critical of others rather than ourselves, when in actuality there really are very basic similarities between humans and the purely fictional alien types in "Star Trek." Thus, our human weaknesses are sometimes more easily glimpsed when we see others exhibiting this kind of behavior. Additionally, there were a lot of dealings with alien cultures in "Star Trek," and knowing something about many of those aliens may clarify certain concepts for the reader when we again encounter these creatures.

Of all the aliens portrayed in the program, the ones we learned the most about were the Vulcans, mainly because the *Enterprise* had a Vulcan science officer, Mr. Spock. We learn of

Vulcans, their characteristics and philosophy through Spock and his associates, and at times we feel frustrated by the almost saint-like, perfectly controlled Vulcans. Understandably, then, we must also learn of their shortcomings.

The importance of the Vulcan viewpoint can be appreciated when we become aware that the greatest statement "Star Trek" made in the area of human prejudice was summed up in the Vulcan philosophy of IDIC (Infinite Diversity in Infinite Combinations)—a philosophy which holds that we must learn to appreciate and cherish the differences in others rather than judging them on appearances alone.

"I am pleased to see that we have differences. May we together become greater than the sum of both of us."

Surak of Vulcan, "The Savage Curtain,"
stardate 5906.4.
In Surak's time, they did not know
of Earthmen, yet he is delighted in
the differences humans have from Vulcans.

"A Vulcan can no sooner be disloyal than he can exist without breathing."

Kirk, "The Menagerie,"
stardate 3012.4.
Kirk emphatically replies to Miss Piper
regarding Spock's inbred loyalty—past
and present.

"Vulcans worship peace above all."

McCoy, "Return to Tomorrow,"
stardate 4768.3.
McCoy states basic Vulcan philosophy.

"The glory of creation is in its infinite diversity."
"And in the way our differences combine to create
meaning and beauty."

Dr. Miranda Jones and Spock, "Is
There In Truth No Beauty?"
stardate 5630.8.
The Vulcan philosophy of IDIC (Infinite
Diversity from Infinite Combinations).
The Medusans have evolved into a race
of beings who are formless, so utterly
hideous that the sight of them brings
total madness to any human who sees one.
Spock and Dr. Miranda Jones are both
excited by the prospects of working with,
and learning from, this unusual life form,
and a certain amount of jealousy can be
detected between them regarding the
assignment with the Medusan Ambassador,
Kollos. By the end of the story, they
have resolved their differences, and
have a fuller understanding of IDIC.

"Emotions are alien to me. I'm a scientist."

Spock, "This Side of Paradise,"
stardate 3417.3.
Leila Kalomi has asked Spock to try
to understand the feelings of the
people of Omicron Ceti III.

" . . . Vulcans believe peace should not depend on
force."

Amanda, Spock's mother, "Journey to Babel,"
stardate 3842.3.
Amanda succinctly states Vulcan
philosophy.

"Vulcans do not approve of violence."

Spock, "Journey to Babel,"
stardate 3842.4.
When McCoy comments that Sarek (Spock's
father) is the most likely suspect in
the killing of the Tellarite Ambassador,
Spock takes exception to this statement.

*"I have heard of Vulcan integrity and personal
honor. There is a well-known saying, or is it a myth,
that Vulcans are incapable of lying."*

Romulan Commander, "The *Enterprise* Incident,"
stardate 5027.3.
The Romulan Commander asks this of
Spock in order for her to determine
the true intention of the *Enterprise*'s
mission.

*"The combination of a number of things to make
existence worthwhile."*
"Yes . . . philosophy of 'nome,' meaning 'All.'"

Spock and Lincoln, "The Savage Curtain,"
stardate 5906.4.
Spock states a basic part of Vulcan
philosophy.

*"Pain is a thing of the mind. The mind can be
controlled."*

Spock, "Operation—Annihilate!"
stardate 3287.2.
With Vulcan techniques, Spock is able
to control the pain caused by the
creatures.

Romulan Commander, Mr. Spock—
THE ENTERPRISE INCIDENT

"It (being a Vulcan) means to adopt a philosophy, a way of life which is logical and beneficial. We cannot disregard that philosophy merely for personal gain, no matter how important that gain might be."

Spock, "Journey to Babel,"
stardate 3842.4.
Spock comments to his mother, Amanda,
on how strongly the Vulcan philosophy
is within him, even to the point that
he could be responsible for the death
of his father.

"We shield it (the Vulcan mating rite) with ritual and custom shrouded in antiquity. You humans have no conception. It strips our minds from us. It brings a madness which rips away the veneer of civilization. It is the pon farr—the time of mating."

Spock, "Amok Time,"
stardate 3372.7.
Spock reveals to his captain the reason
for his unusual behavior.

"We have always fought. We must; we are hunters . . . tracking and taking what we need. There are poor planets in the Klingon systems . . . we must push outward if we are to survive."

Mara, the wife of the Klingon Commander, "Day of the Dove,"
stardate unknown.
Mara tells Kirk why Klingons are an
aggressive people.

"I suppose most of us overlook that fact that even Vulcans aren't indestructible."

Kirk, "Amok Time,"
stardate 3372.7.
Kirk, seeing Spock's deteriorating
condition, grants immediate shore leave
on Vulcan for his first officer.

Mr. Spock, Captain Kirk
AMOK TIME

"Vulcans never bluff."

Spock, "The Doomsday Machine,"
stardate 4202.1.
Spock states this to Commodore Decker,
who at first thinks Spock is bluffing
when he says he will place the Commodore
under arrest.

"Too much love is dangerous."
"Cupid's arrow kills Vulcans."

Dionyd and Eraclitus (Platonians),
"Plato's Stepchildren,"
stardate 5784.3.
Spock's resistance to emotion has
deteriorated, and the Platonians are
ridiculing him about his state of mind.

*"On my planet, to rest is to rest—to cease using
energy. To me, it is quite illogical to run up and
down on green grass, using energy, instead of
saving it."*

Spock, "Shore Leave,"
stardate 3025.2.
Spock does not wish shore leave.

*"As a Vulcan you will study it (Romulan society). As
a human, you would find ways to appreciate it."*

Romulan Commander, "The *Enterprise* Incident,"
stardate 5027.3.
The Romulan Commander has amorous feelings
toward Mr. Spock, and she hopes to
convince him of the many advantages of
her world.

"I object to intellect without discipline; I object to power without constructive purpose."

Spock, "The Squire of Gothos,"
stardate 2124.5.
Spock dislikes Trelane for his
childish actions.

"Fascinating is a word I use for the unexpected."

Spock, "The Squire of Gothos,"
stardate 2124.5.
Spock replies to McCoy that the charade
is interesting, but certainly not
fascinating.

"Hope—I always thought that was a human failing, Mr. Spock."
"True, Doctor. Constant exposure does result in a certain degree of contamination."

McCoy and Spock, "The Gamesters of Triskelion,"
stardate 3211.7.
Spock and McCoy go at it, true to their
usual form.

"In the distant past Vulcans killed to win their mates."
"And they still go mad at this time. Perhaps the price they pay for having no emotions the rest of the time."

Kirk and McCoy, "Amok Time,"
stardate 3372.7.
The two of them reflect on the Vulcan
ceremony of *Koon-Ut-Kal-If-Fee*.

"Their (the Klingon) empire is made up of conquered worlds. They take what they want by arms and force."

Kirk, "Friday's Child,"
stardate 3497.2.
Kirk states to Akaar the Capellan the
Klingon's belief in violence and terror.

"We Klingons believe as you do—the sick should die. Only the strong should live."

Kras the Klingon, "Friday's Child,"
stardate 3497.2.
In attempting to gain the support of
the Capellans, Kras cites the similarities
between Capellan and Klingon beliefs.

"I thought my people would grow tired of killing. But you were right, they see it is easier than trading. And it has its pleasures. I feel it myself. Like the hunt, but with richer rewards."

Apella, leader of Neural's village
people, "A Private Little War,"
stardate 4211.8.
Apella comments that his village
people, like the Klingons, their mentors,
enjoy killing and violence.

"We do not colonize. We conquer. We rule. There is no other way for us."

Rojan the Kelvan, "By Any Other Name,"
stardate 4657.5.
Rojan tells Kirk the basic philosophy
of the Kelvans.

"Romulan women are not like Vulcan females. We are not dedicated to pure logic and the sterility of non-emotion."

Romulan Commander, "The *Enterprise* Incident,"
stardate 5027.3.
The Romulan Commander informs Spock
about some of the characteristics of Romulan women.

"At least we'll be away from all this openness. No, this is too strange for us. We are creatures of outer space. Soon, we will be safe in the comforting closeness of walls."

Rojan the Kelvan, "By Any Other Name,"
stardate 4657.5.
Rojan and his crew, having taken over
the *Enterprise*, long for the comforts
of their home.

"Captain, we can control the Federation as easily as we can control you. The fate of the inferior in any galaxy."

Rojan the Kelvan, "By Any Other Name,"
stardate 4657.5.
Rojan replies to Kirk that the Kelvans
are superior to his Federation and all
their resources.

"Our people are warriors, often savage, but we are also many other pleasant things."

Romulan Commander, "The *Enterprise* Incident,"
stardate 5027.3.
The Romulan Commander attempts to
entice Mr. Spock into an appreciation
of Romulans and their culture.

"They're offering you a chance for combat. They consider it more pleasurable than love."

McCoy, "Friday's Child,"
stardate 3497.2.
McCoy cautions Kirk about a custom
the Capellans practice.

"We found them totally uninterested in medical aid or hospitals. They believe that only the strong should survive."

McCoy, "Friday's Child,"
stardate 3497.2.
McCoy explains to Scott a fundamental
belief of the Capellans.

"This troubled planet (Ardana) is a place of most violent contrasts—those who receive the rewards are totally separated for those who shoulder the burdens. It is not a wise leadership."

Spock, "The Cloud Minders,"
stardate 5818.4.
Spock perceives the inequities between
the peoples of Ardana.

"We believe men should fight their own battles. Only the weak will die."

Proconsul Marcus Claudius, "Bread and Circuses,"
stardate 4041.2.
Claudius tells Kirk the role of the
arena is that each man fights his
own battle. He may not help his friend.

"Tellarites do not argue for reasons; they simply argue."

Sarek of Vulcan, "Journey to Babel,"
stardate 3842.4.
Tellarites are feisty people known throughout the Federation
as being argumentative for no good
reason.

Ambassador Sarek of Vulcan—
JOURNEY TO BABEL

"To us, violence is unthinkable."

Ayleborne of Organia, "Errand of Mercy,"
stardate 3201.7.
The Organians have prevented violence between the Klingons
and the Federation.

*"A truly advanced planet wouldn't use force. They
wouldn't come here in strange alien forms."*

Gary Seven, "Assignment Earth,"
stardate unknown.
Seven is trying to reason with Roberta
about his good intentions.

Ayelbourne of Organia—
ERRAND OF MERCY

CHAPTER THREE

EMOTION AND LOGIC

To Mr. Spock, emotion and logic are as far apart from each other as the Earth is from the planet Vulcan. However, we have included these two topics in the same chapter because to us they are so interconnected that one can't be appreciated without the counterpoint of the other. Indeed, Mr. Spock carried this dichotomy within himself, his hybrid nature tending to make him a more astute observer than a pure-bred Vulcan could ever be.

Throughout the entire series, emotion versus logic oftentimes became the focal point of many a heated debate between the logical Spock, and the warm, humanistic, very emotional Chief Medical Officer, Dr. McCoy. The two of them could be counted on, in any given episode, to have at least one disagreement that made it plain to all on which side they resided.

In addition, emotion and logic are good reference points for observing the human race, especially when commentaries on these topics are given by the extraterrestrial First Officer. He often pointed out how we humans were victimized by our own emotions, when logic could have easily solved our problem.

"Sometimes a feeling is all we humans have to go on."

Kirk, "A Taste of Armageddon,"
stardate 3193.9.
Kirk tries to explain why he acted
out of emotion, which the logical
Mr. Spock has difficulty comprehending.

"Joy can be many things."

Dr. Miranda Jones, "Is There In Truth No Beauty?"
stardate 5630.7.
Miranda relates that she spent four
years on Vulcan studying mental discipline.
McCoy replies that Vulcan is not his
idea of fun, which prompted Miranda's
reply.

"The release of emotion is what keeps us healthy. Emotionally healthy, that is."
"That may be, Doctor. However, I have noted that the healthy release of emotion is frequently unhealthy for those closest to you."

McCoy and Spock, "Plato's Stepchildren,"
stardate 5784.3.
Spock has been forced to display emotion
by the Platonians, and McCoy seeks to
allay Spock's embarrassment.

"Compassion—that's the one thing no machine ever had. Maybe it's the one thing that keeps men ahead of them."

McCoy, "The Ultimate Computer,"
stardate 4731.3.
Kirk gambled on the human compassion of Commodore
Robert Wesley when he kept the
Enterprise shields down—something
a computer running the ship wouldn't
have done.

"What is it in you humans that requires an overwhelming display of emotion in a situation such as this? Two men pursue the only reasonable course of action indicated, and yet you feel that something else is necessary."

Spock, "That Which Survives,"
stardate unknown.
Scott tells Spock that he might at
least say "thank you" for his having
saved the *Enterprise*.

"You thought I was taking your woman away from you. You're jealous. You tried to kill me with your bare hands. Would a Kelvan do that? Would he have to? You're reacting with the emotions of a human. You are human."

Kirk, "By Any Other Name,"
stardate 4657.5.
Kirk points out to Rojan that he and
the other Kelvans have become human
through their form and actions, and
they would be too alien to the normal
Kelvan to be understood.

"One does not thank logic."

Sarek of Vulcan, "Journey to Babel,"
stardate 3842.4.
Sarek explains that his son, Spock, acted
in the only manner open to him in
saving his life, and therefore thanking
him would not be necessary.

"This is loneliness. What a bitter thing ... it's so sad.
How do you bear it, this loneliness?"

Commissioner Nancy Hedford/Companion, "Metamorphosis,"
stardate 3220.3.
The Companion has taken human form and
begins to sense something of human
emotions.

"What is loneliness?"
"It is thirst ... it is a flower, dying in a desert ... "

Reena Kapec and Flint, "Requiem for Methuselah,"
stardate 5843.7.
Flint asks Reena the android if she has
been lonely after her request to meet
the humans.

"Do you know what it's like to be alone, really
alone ... ? (I was given) weapons, a shelter,
food—everything I needed to live—except
companionship ... to send me here alone—if that is
not death, what is?"

Zarabeth of Sarpeidon, "All Our Yesterdays,"
stardate 5943.9.
Zarabeth has been banished to live
out her years in solitude.

Mr. Spock, Arabeth of Sarpeidon, Dr. Leonard McCoy—
ALL OUR YESTERDAYS

"What is it like to feel pain?"
"It is like ... when you see that the people have no
hope for happiness ... you feel great despair ... your
heart is heavy because you know you can do
nothing ... pain is like that."

Hodin and Odona of Gideon, "The Mark of Gideon,"
stardate 5423.4.
Odona's father, from a planet of people
who have never felt pain, asks what it
is like as she lays dying.

"Jealousy has often been a motive for murder."

Kirk, "Wolf in the Fold,"
stardate 3614.9.
Kirk is trying to clear Scott by
finding another possible motive for the
murder of the belly dancer, Kara.

"You humans have that emotional need to express
gratitude. You're welcome, I believe, is the correct
response. However, Doctor, you must remember that
I am entirely motivated by logic."

Spock, "Bread and Circuses,"
stardate 4041.2.
McCoy has just thanked Spock for saving
his life.

"Offense is a human emotion."

Sarek of Vulcan, "Journey to Babel,"
stardate 3842.3.
Sarek's terse remark to Kirk when he
attempts to apologize.

" ... motivations of passion or gain—those are reasons for murder."

Shras, the Andorian Ambassador, "Journey to Babel,"
stardate 3842.2.
Spock discusses the logic in the murder
of Gav and the attack on Kirk with Shras.
Shras suggests that logic may not be
the motivation.

"Anger is a relative state."

Spock, "Wolf in the Fold,"
stardate 3615.4.
Spock, in questioning Morla (an
Argelian), attempts to determine the
extent of his anger.

"Worry is a human emotion."

Spock, "Journey to Babel,"
stardate 3842.4.
Spock reminds Kirk he is a Vulcan, and
accepts what has happened to Sarek, his
father (heart attack), and continues to
perform his duty without any interrup-
tion.

"Deriving sustenance from emotion is not unknown in the galaxy. And fear is among the strongest and most violent of the emotions."

Spock, "Wolf in the Fold,"
stardate 3615.4.
It has been determined that the alien
entity feeds on fear.

"Desperation is a highly emotional state of mind."

Kirk, "The Galilio Seven,"
stardate 2822.3.
Kirk teases Spock for exhibiting the
human emotion of desperation in saving
the Galileo Seven crew.

"Insults are effective only where emotion is present."

Spock, "Who Mourns for Adonais?"
stardate 3468.1.
Spock reminds Apollo of the god Pan—
who always bored him. Therefore, Apollo
requests that Spock remain behind.

*"There's a certain inefficiency in constantly
questioning me on things you've already made up
your mind about."*

Spock, "The Corbomite Maneuver,"
stardate 1514.0.
Kirk knows his course of action requires
that he seek out and contact the alien
life now facing them, but to reassure
himself, he asks Spock's advice. Spock
caustically replies.

*"Monsters come in many forms. And do you know
the greatest monster of them all? Guilt."*

McCoy, "Obsession,"
stardate 3620.7.
Kirk is feeling remorse for not having
killed the creature twelve years ago.

"We humans are full of unpredictable emotions that logic cannot solve."

Kirk, "What Are Little Girls Made Of?"
stardate 2712.4.
Kirk explains the weaknesses of humans
to the android Ruk.

"Threats are illogical."

Sarek, "Journey to Babel,"
stardate 3842.3.
Gav, the Ambassador from Tellar, quarrels
openly with Sarek, who curtly replies.

"Respect is a rational process."

McCoy, "The Galileo Seven,"
stardate 2822.3.
McCoy admonishes Spock that his logical
approach of frightening the creatures
with their superior weapons was incorrect
because these lower life forms reacted
with anger.

"It would be illogical to assume that all conditions remain stable."

Spock, "The *Enterprise* Incident,"
stardate 5027.3.
The Romulan Commander has told Spock
of the forbidden corridor, but she
hopes to woo Spock over to the
Romulan side, thus removing all restrictions.

"Logic and practical information do not seem to apply here."
"You admit that?"
"To deny the facts would be illogical, Doctor."

Spock and McCoy, "A Piece of the Action,"
stardate unknown.
Spock and McCoy go at it again! Spock
admits that it is logical to be illogical
in this situation.

"You can't evaluate a man by logic alone."

McCoy, "I, Mudd,"
stardate 4513.3.
Spock believes Norman is behaving
logically, while McCoy feels there's
something strange about him.

"Life and death are seldom logical."
"But attaining a desired goal always is."

McCoy and Spock, "The Galileo Seven,"
stardate 2821.7.
Spock must choose who will have to stay
behind on the planet.

"It would be illogical to kill without reason."

Spock, "Journey to Babel,"
stardate 3842.4.
Spock makes a statement in defense of
Sarek, his father.

"Can you imagine how life could be improved if we could do away with jealousy, greed, hate . . ."
"It can also be improved by eliminating love, tenderness, sentiment—the other side of the coin."

Dr. Roger Corby and Kirk, "What Are Little Girls Made Of?"
stardate 2712.4.
Corby tries to convince Kirk that
by transferring men's "souls" into
android bodies, all human problems
would be eliminated. Sarcastically,
Kirk counters his argument.

"Without facts, the decision cannot be made logically. You must rely on your human intuition."

Spock, "Assignment Earth,"
stardate unknown.
Spock does not have the data needed
for him to execute the delicate
maneuver to detonate the warhead. He
tells Kirk to use his intuition to make
the decision about Gary Seven's proper
intentions.

"You say you are lying. But if everything you say is a lie, then you are telling the truth. You cannot tell the truth, because everything you say is a lie. You lie, you tell the truth . . . but you cannot, for you lie."

Norman the android, "I Mudd,"
stardate 4513.3.
Kirk attempts to trap the androids into
trying to solve an ancient Möbius strip
logic trick.

"It is more rational to sacrifice one life than six."

Spock, "The Galileo Seven,"
stardate 2822.3.
Spock, concerned and in command, states
that someone will have to be left
behind in order for the craft to lift off.

Allice 11; Alice 8; Norman, the Android—
I, MUDD

CHAPTER FOUR

WAR AND PEACE

By the twenty-third century, war will be a thing of the past for the planet Earth.

The human race will make it after all!

With so much violence and unrest in our own time, this hopeful, optimistic view of our future is a strong drawing card for the twentieth-century Earthlings who fret over the possibility some trigger-happy maniac may at any moment push the button, launch the bomb, and blow our planet into space dust.

Unfortunately, although Earth is war-free, the galaxy is not. The *Enterprise* often encounters potentially explosive situations, placing the sometimes cool, sometimes impassioned James T. Kirk, in a position to defuse things before they get worse. And the Captain does an admirable job, spreading the word among the inhabitants of the Milky Way that the representatives of Earth and the United Federation of Planets (UFP) believe peace is the way.

"I think that one day they're going to take all this money that we spend now on war and death—"
"And make them spend it on life."

Edith Keeler and Kirk, "The City On The Edge of Forever,"
stardate unknown.
The two of them are contemplating the
future of Earth's people.

"Our missions are peaceful—not for conquest. When we do battle, it is only because we have no choice."

Kirk, "The Squire of Gothos,"
stardate 2124.5.
Trelane asks Kirk to tell of his
battles and missions of conquest.

"We fight only when there is no other choice. We prefer the ways of peaceful contact."

Kirk, "Spectre of the Gun,"
stardate 4385.3.
The Melkotians are amazed that the
humans did not wish to fight.

"Only a fool fights in a burning house."

Kang, the Klingon Commander, "Day of the Dove,"
stardate unknown.
Kang realizes that if it were not for
the common cause truce with Kirk, the
alien would have taken control over
them forever.

"Our way is peace."

Septimus, the Son Worshipper, "Bread and Circuses,"
stardate 4040.7.
Septimus is pleased Flavius has not
shown his barbaric nature by sparing
the lives of Kirk and the landing party.

Kang, the Klingon Commander—
DAY OF THE DOVE

"Men of peace usually are (brave)."

Spock, "The Savage Curtain,"
stardate 5906.5.
Spock replies to Kirk's remark that
Surak is a brave man.

"No one talks peace unless he's ready to back it up with war."
"He talks of peace if it is the only way to live."

Colonel Green and Surak of Vulcan, "The Savage Curtain,"
stardate 5906.5.
Green refuses to believe that the pro-
posal of peace is legitimate. Surak
attempts to assure him it is.

"There's another way to survive. Mutual trust—and help."

Kirk, "Day of the Dove,"
stardate unknown.
Mara, the Klingon Commander's wife,
has stated that the Klingons are from
a system of poor planets, and they must
push outward if they are to survive.
Kirk suggests an alternative.

"If some day we are defeated, well, war has its fortunes, good and bad."

Commander Kor, "Errand of Mercy,"
stardate 3201.7.
The Klingons' goal is to rule the galaxy,
but they are realistic about war in
general.

"It's (war is) instinctive. But the instinct can be fought. We're human beings with the blood of a million savage years on our hands! But we can stop it. We can admit that we're killers ... but we're not going to kill today. That's all it takes! Knowing that we're not going to kill today!"

Kirk, "A Taste of Armageddon,"
stardate 3193.0.
Kirk defends humanity when Anan 7
believes there can never be peace.

"Actual war is a very messy business. Very, very messy business."

Kirk, "A Taste of Armageddon,"
stardate 3193.0.
With the Eminians' neat little computer
war over, Kirk conveys the realities
of war.

"War isn't a good life, but it's life."

Kirk, "A Private Little War,"
stardate 4211.8.
Kirk knows that Tyree, the leader of
Neural's hill tribe, won't fight, and
he hopes he will at least defend himself.

"'You Earth people glorified organized violence for forty centuries. But you imprison those who employ it privately."

Spock, "Dagger of the Mind,"
stardate 2715.1.
Spock notes the differences between
war and individual crimes of violence.

"Another war . . . must it always be so? How many comrades have we lost in this way? . . . Obedience. Duty. Death, and more death . . . "

Romulan Commander, "Balance of Terror,"
stardate 1709.2.
The Commander questions the ideology
of his society.

"There's no honorable way to kill, no gentle way to destroy. There is nothing good in war. Except its ending."

Abraham Lincoln, "The Savage Curtain,"
stardate 5906.5.
Lincoln regrets having sent men to their
deaths in the four years of civil war
during his office.

" . . . bacteriological warfare . . . hard to believe we were once foolish enough to play around with that."

McCoy, "The Omega Glory,"
stardate unknown.
McCoy says the disease on this planet
resembles one developed by Earth in
the 1990's during bacteriological
warfare experiments.

"Those who hate and fight must stop themselves—otherwise it is not stopped."

Spock, "Day of the Dove,"
stardate unknown.
Spock restrains McCoy who is trying to
end the fighting between the crew of
the *Enterprise* and the Klingons.

Abraham Lincoln—
THE SAVAGE CURTAIN

"War is never imperative."

McCoy, "Balance of Terror,"
stardate 1709.2.
Spock thinks the Romulans, offshoots
from Vulcans centuries ago, must still
carry warlike traits and should be
stopped immediately by attacking.

*"Another Armenia, Belgium . . . the weak innocents
who always seem to be located on a natural
invasion route."*

Kirk, "Errand of Mercy,"
stardate 3198.4.
Organia is a planet of strategic
importance to the Federation as well
as the Klingon Empire.

"No one wants war."

Kirk, "Errand of Mercy,"
stardate 3201.7.
Kirk is still convinced he and Kor can
best settle their own affairs without
interference from the Organians.

*"Death. Destruction. Disease. Horror. That's what war
is all about. That's what makes it a thing to be
avoided."*

Kirk, "A Taste of Armageddon,"
stardate 3193.0.
Kirk tries to explain to Anan what
real war is, not a computer war like
the one they've been fighting for 500
years.

Kor—
ERRAND OF MERCY

"Peace was the way."

Kirk, "The City On The Edge of Forever,"
stardate unknown.
McCoy's inadvertant passage through
the time vortex has altered the course
of Earth's history. Spock's tricorder
has picked up the Time Guardian's pre-
sentation of all that now is. In playing
back this new version of history, Spock
discovers that Hitler won the Second
World War, and that Edith Keeler is
directly responsible for this different
outcome.
As the founder of the peace movement,
she delayed America's entry into the
war long enough for Germany to develop
the A-Bomb and gain control of the
world. Now, Kirk sadly admits to the
fact that although Edith was correct
in her peaceful ideals, history must
be set back on its true course. Edith
must die as she should have.

*"The face of war has never changed. Surely it is
more logical to heal than kill."*

Surak of Vulcan, "The Savage Curtain,"
stardate 5906.5.
When Kirk points out that circumstances
were different in Surak's time, Surak
nevertheless defends his desire to
make peace with their opponents.

CHAPTER FIVE

THE MILITARY

Starfleet is the armed security force of the United Federation of Planets. It is a defensive, peace-keeping organization which employs military procedures. There are several classifications of vessels, including heavy cruisers like the U.S.S. *Enterprise,* passenger liners and transports.

The *Enterprise*'s mission is one of peaceful exploration, although she does carry arms and is quite capable of defense, or even—should it be deemed necessary—attack.

The officers of the starship are graduates of Starfleet Academy, a kind of twenty-third century version of Annapolis, and indeed the close parallel between naval protocol and Starfleet is not entirely by chance. Naval tradition is evident aboard the *Enterprise,* and final command authority rests with her Captain, James Tiberius Kirk—who is a direct outgrowth of Gene Roddenberry's fondness for C. S. Forester's character, Horatio Hornblower.

In a sense, Kirk is perfectly mated to his ship, although it is not always easy for him to remain in this blissful symbiotic state, and occasionally he has doubts about his own feelings toward the one true love of his life. Yet, in the end, his inner reserve of strength prevails, for although he would prefer not engaging in hostilities and risking his ship, when forced to do so he is a formidable opponent. The *Enterprise* and the safety of her crew are the driving forces in Kirk's life.

"Do you know the one—'All I ask is a tall ship ... and a star to steer her by ... ' You could feel the wind at your back, about you ... the sounds of the sea beneath you. And even if you take away the wind and the water, it's still the same. The ship is yours ... you can feel her ... and the stars are still there."

Kirk, "The Ultimate Computer,"
stardate 4729.4.
Kirk expresses his feelings about
being a starship captain while confiding
in Dr. McCoy.

"I've already got a female to worry about. Her name is the Enterprise.*"*

Kirk, "The Corbomite Maneuver,"
stardate 1514.0.
Kirk is annoyed at the flirtatious
attention he is receiving from Yeoman
Janice Rand.

"I'm a soldier, not a diplomat. I can only tell the truth."

Kirk, "Errand of Mercy,"
stardate 3198.9.
Kirk offers to help the Organians
defend themselves against the Klingons.

"One of the advantages of being a captain is being able to ask for advice without necessarily having to take it."

Kirk, "Dagger of the Mind,"
stardate 2715.2.
Kirk has brought Dr. Helen Noel along
for advice; now he politely refuses to
take it.

"Intuition, however illogical, is recognized as a command prerogative."

Kirk, "Obsession,"
stardate 3620.7.
Kirk attempts to rationalize his actions
to Spock and McCoy regarding his
obsession with the creature.

"A star captain's most solemn oath is that he will give his life, even his entire crew, rather than violate the Prime Directive."

Kirk, "The Omega Glory,"
stardate unknown.
Kirk is dismayed to think that Captain
Ronald Tracy may have violated Starfleet's
Prime Directive.

"The man on top walks a lonely street; the 'chain' of command is often a noose."

McCoy, "The Conscience of the King,"
stardate 2818.9.
Spock has asked him if he has noticed
any strange behavior in the Captain.

"Either one of us, by himself, is expendable. Both of us are not."

Kirk, "The Devil in the Dark,"
stardate 3196.1.
Kirk reminds Spock he is second in
command and because of the dangerous
hunt, they should separate to prevent
possible disaster to both of them.

Mr. Spock, Captain Kirk—
THE DEVIL IN THE DARK

"Computers make excellent and efficient servants, but I have no wish to serve under them. Captain, a starship also runs on loyalty to one man. And nothing can replace it or him."

Spock, "The Ultimate Computer,"
stardate 4729.4.
Spock consoles Kirk, who is feeling
depressed about the possibility of
losing the captaincy to a computer.

"I realize that command does have its fascination, even under circumstances such as these, but I neither enjoy the idea of command, nor am I frightened of it. It simply exists, and I will do whatever logically needs to be done."

Spock, "The Galileo Seven,"
stardate 2812.7.
Spock replies to Dr. McCoy's caustic
remark about the best basis on which
to build a command.

"The only solution is . . . a balance of power. We arm our side exactly that much more. A balance of power—the trickiest, most difficult, dirtiest game of them all. But the only one that preserves both sides."

Kirk, "A Private Little War,"
stardate 4211.8.
The Klingons have armed one side and
upset the balance of power on the planet.
Kirk, his judgment obscured by the
spell of Nona the Witchwoman, sees equal
arms as the only solution to this dilemma.

"You speak of courage. Obviously you do not know the difference between courage and foolhardiness. Always it is the brave ones who die, the soldiers."

Kor, the Klingon Commander, "Errand of Mercy,"
stardate 3201.7.
Kor criticizes Kirk for attempting to
arouse the Organians to fight.

"First study the enemy. Seek weakness."

Romulan Commander, "Balance of Terror,"
stardate 1709.2.
The Commander believes that this is
the reason that the *Enterprise* has not
attacked.

"You are an excellent tactician, Captain. You let your second-in-command attack while you sit and watch for weakness."

Khan Noonian Singh, "Space Seed,"
stardate 3141.9.
Khan, annoyed by the natural curiosity
of the *Enterprise*'s officers to know
about his past, taunts Captain Kirk.

"Four thousand throats may be cut in one night by a running man."

Klingon soldier, "Day of the Dove,"
stardate unknown.
The Klingons are talking about how
they can take over the *Enterprise,*
even though there are only forty of them
versus over 400 *Enterprise* crew members.

"Conquest is easy. Control is not."

Kirk, "Mirror, Mirror,"
stardate unknown.
Kirk replies to the Alternate Spock's
statement that terror must be main-
tained or the empire is doomed.

Khan Noonian Singh—
SPACE SEED

"If I can have honesty, it's easier to overlook mistakes."

Kirk, "Space Seed,"
stardate 3141.9.
Kirk replies to Lt. Marla McGivers
regarding her conduct with the landing
party earlier.

"Power is danger."

The Centurion, "Balance of Terror,"
stardate 1709.2.
The Centurion, speaking as a friend to the
Romulan Commander, warns him to be
aware that the officer he has demoted
for an infraction of the rules has
powerful and influential friends.

"Military secrets are the most fleeting of all."

Spock, "The *Enterprise* Incident,"
stardate 5027.4.
Spock informs the Romulan Commander he
is aware that the Romulans will soon learn
to penetrate the cloaking device.

"Leave bigotry in your quarters; there's no room for it on the bridge."

Kirk, "Balance of Terror,"
stardate 1709.2.
Kirk criticizes Lt. Andrew Stiles for
his attitude in the performance of his
duty.

CHAPTER SIX

MEN AND WOMEN

There is a humorous story which "Star Trek" creator Gene Roddenberry often relates. At the time the program concept was submitted to the NBC network, the format called for a starship crew of fifty percent men and fifty percent women. Although in the mid-60's there wasn't one woman in the space program training to be an astronaut, Gene was convinced the future of space travel would surely include total equality of the sexes.

Unfortunately, the network didn't buy this, at least not for their show. They took the position that this concept simply could not be included in what essentially was a family television program. The ship's crew lived in tight quarters, and it would certainly look like there was a lot of fooling around going on up there in space! Reluctantly, a compromise was struck whereby one-third of the crew would be composed of women. "I figured that one-third healthy women could easily handle all the men if necessary!"

But if Roddenberry couldn't get what he wanted one way, he would try another. He saw to it that women were given important leadership roles, such as commanders and doctors. Yet he still delighted in the differences between the sexes; for although men and women of the twenty-third century have achieved equality, they are still not necessarily the same, and in the spirit of IDIC, each sex is appreciated for its differences.

In some cases, even Gene Roddenberry could not rise above the traditional way of thinking—occasionally exhibiting just a tinge of good old-fashioned chauvanism, perhaps the show's only drawback. In retrospect, it's a point he's willing to concede. After all, no program, not even "Star Trek," is perfect!

"The idea of male and female are universal constants."

Kirk, "Metamorphosis,"
stardate 3219.8.
Zefrem Cochrane is confused as to
why the translator projects the
Companion's voice as female.

"Is not that the nature of men and women—that the pleasure is in the learning of each other?"

Natira, the High Priestess of Yonada,
"For the World is Hollow and I Have Touched the Sky,"
stardate 5476.3.
Natira has asked Dr. McCoy to stay on
Yonada as her mate, to which McCoy
replies that they are strangers.

"There's only one kind of woman...."
"Or man, for that matter."
"You either believe in yourself or you don't."

Kirk and Harry Mudd, "Mudd's Women,"
stardate 1330.1.
The women have been
duped into believing that their beauty
was derived from a pill, when true beauty
really comes from inside.

Harry Mudd, Captain Kirk—
MUDD'S WOMEN

"This cultural mystique surrounding the biological function—you realize humans are overly preoccupied with the subject."

Kelinda the Kelvan, "By Any Other Name,"
stardate 4658.9.
Kelinda is an alien in a human body
attempting to understand her strange
new feelings.

"Earth—mother of the most beautiful women in the universe."

Apollo, "Who Mourns for Adonais?"
stardate 3468.1.
The god Apollo has just set eyes upon
Lt. Carolyn Palamas.

"Women professionals do tend to over-compensate."

Dr. Elizabeth Dehaver, "Where No Man Has Gone Before,"
stardate 1312.9.
Elizabeth replies to Lt. Commander
Mitchell regarding her "bedside
manner" as a doctor. Mitchell, who
is chauvanistic, would prefer her to
be more womanly.

"Extreme feminine beauty is always disturbing."

Spock, "The Cloud Minders,"
stardate 5818.4.
Droxine of Stratos has asked if there
is nothing which can disturb the Vulcan
seven-year mating cycle.

"Behind every great man, there is a woman—urging him on."

Harry Mudd, "I, Mudd,"
stardate 4513.3.
Harry was a hen-pecked husband. His
wife kept urging him into outer space,
not that she meant to, but with her
continual, eternal, confounded nagging,
Harry was pushed further and further out
into space.

"A woman should have compassion."

Kirk, "Catspaw,"
stardate 3018.2.
Kirk explains to Sylvia the sorceress
what a real woman's feelings should be.

"There is an old custom among my people. When a woman saves a man's life, he is grateful."

Nona, the Kanutu witchwoman, "A Private Little War,"
stardate 4211.8.
Nona quotes an old custom to Kirk
because she has ulterior motives.

"Worlds may change, galaxies disintegrate, but a woman always remains a woman."

Kirk, "The Conscience of the King,"
stardate 2818.9.
Lenore Karidian asks Kirk if women
have changed as a result of starship
duty.

"Women are more easily and more deeply terrified . . . generating more sheer horror than the male of the species."

Spock, "Wolf in the Fold,"
stardate 3615.4.
Spock believes this is why women are
being preyed upon by the unknown entity.

"That unit is a woman."
"A mass of conflicting impulses."

Spock and Nomad, "The Changeling,"
stardate 3541.9.
The computer Nomad has just absorbed all the knowledge
from Uhura's mind.

"It is undignified for a woman to play servant to a man who is not hers."

Spock, "Amok Time,"
stardate 3372.7.
Spock comments to an incredulous Kirk
after throwing Nurse Chapel out
of his quarters for doing her job.

"Men will always be men—no matter where they are."

Harry Mudd, "Mudd's Women,"
stardate 1329.8.
Mudd comments on the positive reaction
by the *Enterprise* crewmen to his female
cargo. Their desirability, intrigue
and presence are fully appreciated.

"There are certain things men must do to remain men."

Kirk, "The Ultimate Computer,"
stardate 4729.4.
Kirk fears that placing a computer in
control of the *Enterprise* may eventually
result in his not being needed.

"I have never understood the female capacity to avoid a direct answer to any question."

Spock, "This Side of Paradise,"
stardate 3417.3.
Leila Kalomi has told Spock she will
answer his questions later.

"Oh, that sound of male ego, You travel halfway across the galaxy and it's still the same song."

Eve McHuron, "Mudd's Women,"
stardate 1330.1.
Eve has been getting to know her new
mail-order husband.

"A princess should not be afraid—not with a brave knight to protect her."

McCoy, "Shore Leave,"
stardate 3025.3.
McCoy, feeling romantic and virile,
vows to protect Yeoman Tonia Barrow
from any harm.

CHAPTER SEVEN

LOVE

"Star Trek" presents a world of optimism, hope and love in the twenty-third century. Optimism and hope provide the *faith* in this future; love is the *promise*. Love is universal and the devotion and affection beings have for one another is the foundation on which the future is built. "Star Trek" assures us that love is alive and prospering in the twenty-third century.

"Love is the most important thing on Earth—especially to a man and a woman."

Kirk, "The Gamesters of Triskelion,"
stardate 3259.2.
Shahna, one of the Thralls, asks Kirk
what the word "love" means.

"Do you love the man? ... Is he important to you? More important than anything? Is he—as though he were a part of you?"

Kirk, "Metamorphosis,"
stardate 3220.3.
Kirk defines "love" for the Companion.

"You'll learn something about men and women—the way they're supposed to be. Caring for each other, being happy with each other, being good to each other. That's what we call love. You'll like that alot."

Kirk, "The Apple,"
stardate 3715.6.
Without Vaal, the people of the planet
can learn about love.—

Mr. Spock, Captain Kirk, Dr. McCoy, Yeoman
Martha Landon, Mr. Chekov—
THE APPLE

*"Do you know about being with somebody?
Wanting to be? If I had the whole universe, I'd give it
to you. When I see you, I feel like I'm hungry all
over. Do you know how that feels?"*

Charlie Evans, "Charlie X,"
stardate 1535.8.
Charlie expresses his emotions to
Yeoman Janice Rand, who is much older
than he. This is Charlie's first
experience with love.

*"You go slow, be gentle. It's no one-way street—you
know how you feel and that's all. It's how the girl
feels too. Don't press. If the girl feels anything for
you at all, you'll know."*

Kirk, "Charlie X"
stardate 1535.8.
Kirk gives Charlie Evans the benefit
of his years by trying to explain love
and how to handle it.

"Each kiss is as the first."

Miramanee, Kirk's wife, "The Paradise Syndrome,"
stardate 4842.6.
Miramanee is about to die, and she
speaks these last words to Kirk.

"Love sometimes expresses itself in sacrifice."

Kirk, "Metamorphosis,"
stardate 3220.3.
Kirk hopes that the Companion loves
Zefrem Cochrane enough to let him go.

"Humans do claim a great deal for that particular emotion (love)."

Spock, "The Lights of Zetar,"
stardate 5725.6.
Spock considers the possibility that
Scotty's love may have been a motivation
for Lt. Romaine's ability to survive
the Zetars.

"The heart is not a logical organ."

Dr. Janet Wallace, "The Deadly Years,"
stardate 3479.4.
Janet conveys to Kirk that, after all
these years, she is still in love with him.

"It is a human characteristic to love little animals, especially if they're attractive in some way."

McCoy, "The Trouble With Tribbles,"
stardate 4525.6.
McCoy is trying to explain to Spock the
reason tribbles are so appealing to the
rest of the crew.

"What kind of life is that? Not to be loved; never to have shown love."

Commissioner Nancy Hedford, "Metamorphosis,"
stardate 3219.8.
Zefrem Cochrane has been loved by the
Companion, but is prejudiced against
this alien life form. Nancy has never
been loved in her life, and in her
feverish state, admits her unhappiness.

"Oblivion together does not frighten me, beloved."

Thalassa (in Anne Mulhall's body), "Return to Tomorrow,"
stardate 4770.3.
Thalassa knows that she and Sargon
cannot live in Kirk's world, and these
are her parting words to Sargon.

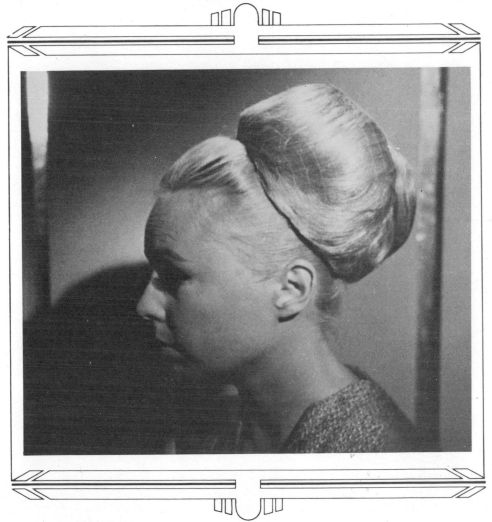

Dr. Janet Wallace—
THE DEADLY YEARS

"...the things love can drive a man to—the ecstasies, the miseries, the broken rules, the desperate chances, the glorious failures, and the glorious victories."

McCoy, "Requiem for Methuselah,"
stardate 5843.7.
McCoy says Spock will never know these
things.

"The sooner our happiness together begins, the longer it will last."

Miramanee, the tribal priestess, "The Paradise Syndrome,"
stardate 4842.6.
Tribal law betroths Miramanee to Kirk,
much to his surprise, and she asks Kirk
if she can name the day they are to be
married.

"The joys of love made her human, and the agonies of love destroyed her."

Spock, "Requiem for Methuselah,"
stardate 5842.8.
Spock rationalizes Reena the android's
"death."

"Too much of anything, even love, isn't necessarily a good thing."

Kirk, "The Trouble With Tribbles,"
stardate 4525.6.
Uhura has stated that tribbles are the
only love money can buy, while Kirk is
beginning to have his doubts about the
virtues of the tribbles.

CHAPTER EIGHT

LIFE AND DEATH

In "Star Trek's" time, life is highly appreciated for the priceless gift that it is. Life is a sacred, mysterious thing, and the sanctity of life is universally cherished.

In a sense, "Star Trek" is a paean to life. The five-year mission of the *Enterprise* states, in part: " . . . to seek out new life . . . " This goal is one of the reasons for the existence of the star-ship, and her crew learns many lessons in the value of all life forms. No matter how minute, bizarre or ugly the creatures encountered, all life forms are to be given credence and acceptance—even such seemingly ugly aliens as the lizard-like Gorn, the frightening-appearing mother Horta and the bizarre Melkots.

If the value of life is prime, the taking of life and causing of death is abhorrent. Death itself is seen as a part of life whose existence must be admitted. The only positive thing "Star

Trek" says about death is that there can be meaningful ones—giving one's life in the line of duty, sacrificing one's self in order to gain the lives of many—these were seen as admirable ways to die. Otherwise, death is tragic, but nevertheless a reality which must be accepted.

"A man either lives life as it happens to him, meets it head-on and licks it, or he turns his back on it and starts to wither away."

Dr. Boyce, "The Menagerie" ("The Cage"),
stardate unknown.
Pike has considered resigning from
the service. Boyce points out that
Pike wouldn't be happy doing anything else.

"The people of Gideon have always believed that life is sacred. That the love of life is the greatest gift . . . we are incapable of destroying or interfering with the creation of that which we love so deeply—life in every form from fetus to developed being."

Hodin of Gideon, "The Mark of Gideon,"
stardate 5423.4.
The leader of Gideon tries to explain
why his planet is so overpopulated.

"To live is always desirable."

Eleen the Capellan, "Friday's Child,"
stardate 3498.9.
Kirk asks if even though she was
prepared to die, does that mean she
wished to die?

Hodin of Gideon—
THE MARK OF GIDEON

"When dreams become more important than reality, you give up travel, building, creating; you even forget how to repair the machines left behind by your ancestors. You just sit living and reliving other lives left behind in the thought records."

Vina, "The Menagerie" ("The Cage"),
stardate unknown.
Vina explains to Captain Pike that
thousands of centuries ago the Talosians
went underground and concentrated on
developing their mental powers.

"Lots of people drink from the wrong bottle sometimes."

Edith Keeler, "The City on the Edge of Forever,"
stardate unknown.
After McCoy thanks Edith Keeler for possibly
saving his life, she does not condemn him for
what she thinks is an alchohol problem, although
he's actually been suffering from an accidental
overdose of Cordrazine.

"We both get the same two kinds of customers—the living and the dying."

Dr. Boyce, "The Menagerie" ("The Cage"),
stardate unknown.
Boyce, who has been giving Pike some
friendly advice over a drink, now
contemplates the similarities between
doctors and bartenders.

Captain Christopher Pike, Vina—
THE MENAGERIE

"There's nothing disgusting about it (the Cloud). It's just another life form, that's all. You get used to those things."

McCoy, "Metamorphosis,"
stardate 3219.8.
Zefrem Cochrane is now disgusted at
learning that the Cloud/Companion loves
him.

"Immortality consists largely of boredom."

Zefrem Cochrane, "Metamorphosis,"
stardate 3219.8.
Cochrane has ceased aging since
landing on the planet decades ago.

"In the strict scientific sense we all feed on death—even vegetarians."

Spock, "Wolf in the Fold,"
stardate 3615.4.
Sybo (an Argelian) has said that the
entity feeds on death. Spock would
like more elaborate information.

"Blast medicine anyway! We've learned to tie into every organ in the human body but one. The brain! The brain is what life is all about."

McCoy, "The Menagerie,"
stardate 3012.4.
McCoy is frustrated by his inability
to reach the active brain of Captain
Pike, imprisoned in a vegetating body.

Zefrem Cochrane—
METAMORPHOSIS

"Suffocating together ... would create heroic camaraderie."

Khan Noonian Singh, "Space Seed,"
stardate 3142.8.
Khan, trying to force the crew to join
him, contemplates their unity.

"Death, when unnecessary, is a tragic thing."

Flint, "Requiem for Methuselah,"
stardate 5843.7.
Flint replies to Reena Kapec's
statement that she is glad Kirk did not
die.

"The sight of death frightens them (Earthmen)."

Kras the Klingon, "Friday's Child,"
stardate 3497.2.
Kras comments to the Capellans, Akaar
and Maab, that his people's beliefs
are similar to theirs, and that the
Earthmen are much different in their
ways.

"There are some things worth dying for."

Kirk, "Errand of Mercy,"
stardate 3201.7.
Kirk and Spock intend to stop the
Klingons from any further takeover of
Organia, knowing the odds are stacked
against them.

"What a terrible way to die."
"There are no good ways."

Sulu and Kirk, "That Which Survives,"
stardate unknown.
Lt. D'Amato has just died by having
every cell in his body disrupted.

*"I'm frequently appalled by the low regard you
Earthmen have for life."*

Spock, "The Galileo Seven,"
stardate 2822.3.
The men want to attack the creatures
on the planet.

*"The games have always strengthened us. Death
becomes a familiar pattern. We don't fear it as you
do."*

Proconsul Marcus Claudius, "Bread and Circuses,"
stardate 4041.2.
Claudius tells Kirk a fundamental belief
of their society regarding death.

*"He gave his life in an attempt to save others. Not
the worst way to go."*

Kirk, "The Doomsday Machine,"
stardate 4202.9.
Matt Decker took a shuttlecraft into
the heart of the robot machine in an
attempt to destroy it and save the
Enterprise.

Captain Kirk—
THE DOOMSDAY MACHINE

CHAPTER NINE

SOCIETY AND GOVERNMENT

General Order No. 1, the "Prime Directive" of Starfleet, states that no representative of the Federation shall interfere with the development of any society or government on any planet. All societies and cultures have the right to determine their own future and way of life without interference from outsiders.

This non-interference directive was actually Gene Roddenberry's means of commenting, in the late 60's, that we hadn't the right to interfere in the affairs of the people of Southeast Asia, or anywhere else for that matter. By putting these convictions into an outer space context, he was indirectly able to express his opinions on things which greatly concerned him.

In this chapter we have expressions of freedom from both the people of Earth and the people of other worlds, confirming our acceptance of their way of life and the choice they have made.

"Liberty and freedom have to be more than just words."

Kirk, "The Omega Glory,"
stardate unknown.
Kirk has shown the people of Omege IV
what they really were fighting for.

"Look at these three words written larger than all the rest, and with a special pride never written before or since—tall words, proudly saying, 'We the people'...these words and the words that follow...must apply to everyone or they mean nothing."

Kirk, "The Omega Glory,"
stardate unknown.
Kirk is addressing the Kohms and Yangs
of the planet Omega IV on the true meaning
of their sacred documents.

"We once were as you are. Spears and arrows. There came a time when our weapons grew faster than our wisdom, and we almost destroyed ourselves. We learned from this to make a rule during all our travels never to cause the same to happen to other worlds...just as a man must grow in his own way and his own time."

Kirk, "A Private Little War,"
stardate 4211.8.
The basic philosohpy of non-interference.
Kirk states this to Nona, who urges
her husband Tyree (leader of Neural's
hill tribe) to obtain more sophisticated
weapons from his friends from space.

"There are certain absolutes, and one of them is the right of humanoids to a free and unchained environment—the right to have conditions which permit growth."
"Another is their right to choose that system which seems to work best for them."

McCoy and Spock, "The Apple,"
stardate 3715.6.
McCoy would like to break the Prime
Directive and interfere with the stagnant
culture on Gamma Trianguli VI.

"Human beings do not survive on bread alone...but on the nourishments of liberty. For what indeed is a man without freedom...naught but a mechanism, trapped in the cogwheels of eternity."

Harry Mudd, "I, Mudd,"
stardate 4513.3.
Mudd argues that the robots have
harmed man by not allowing them
freedom.

"There are many who are uncomfortable with what we have created. It is almost a biological rebellion. A profound revulsion against the planned communities, the programming, the sterilized, artfully balanced atmospheres. They hunger for an Eden, where spring comes."
"We all do. The cave is deep in our memories."

Spock and Kirk, "The Way to Eden,"
stardate 5832.3.
Spock, sympathizing with the dissidents'
cause, explains their philosophy to Kirk.

"All the little things you and I understand and expect from life, such as: equality; kindness; justice...."

Spock, "The Cloud Minders,"
stardate 5818.4.
Droxine of Stratos believes the
Troglytes are inferior, and Spock
believes they understand more than just
violence.

"A species that enslaves other beings is hardly superior—mentally or otherwise."

Kirk, "The Gamesters of Triskelion,"
stardate 3211.7.
The Provider has told Kirk that his
species has evolved into superior beings.

"It's wrong to create a whole race of humans to live as slaves."

Number One, "The Menagerie" ("The Cage"),
stardate unknown.
Number One sets her laser to overload,
preferring to die rather than be a slave.

"To restrict a segment of the population to such hardship is unthinkable in an evolved culture."

Spock, "The Cloud Minders,"
stardate 5818.4.
Kirk and Spock cannot understand the
treatment rendered to the Troglytes
by the Stratos dwellers.

Number One—
THE MENAGERIE

"The highest of all our laws states your world is yours and will always remain yours."

Kirk, "Friday's Child,"
stardate 3497.2.
Kirk states to Akaar the Capellan
the Federation's philosophy of non-
interference.

"I don't think we have the right or the wisdom to interfere, however a planet is evolving."

Kirk, "The Omega Glory,"
stardate unknown.
Kirk replies to Captain Ronald Tracy,
who is trying to justify his violation
of the Prime Directive.

"It is one of our most important laws that none of us may interfere with the affairs of others."

Kirk, "Bread and Circuses,"
stardate 4040.7.
Kirk explains to Septimus (the Son
Worshipper) the Prime Directive of his
governing body, which prohibits the
crew of the *Enterprise* from interfering
in their matters.

"Our people don't believe in slavery."

Kirk, "Bread and Circuses,"
stardate 4040.7.
Septimus the Son Worshipper assumes
that Kirk and his men are slaves like
themselves.

"We are wise enough to know we are wise enough not to interfere with the way of a man or another world."

Kirk, "A Private Little War,"
stardate 4211.8.
The non-interference directive, an
important tenet of the Federation.

"You'll learn to build houses to keep warm. You'll work. . . . Humans have survived under worse conditions. It's a matter of evolution. Give it time."

Kirk, "Spock's Brain,"
stardate 5432.3.
Kirk encourages Kara the Eymorg and
her people to live on the surface
with the Morgs.

"The only tool diplomacy has is language."

Hodin of Gideon, "The Mark of Gideon,"
stardate 5423.4.
Spock had asked that he be allowed to
beam down to the planet Gideon to search
for Kirk. The people of Gideon
conducted the search without Spock,
falsely claiming that Spock's request
was unclearly stated.

"We're free people. We belong to no one."

Kirk, "The Gamesters of Triskelion,"
stardate 3259.2.
The Providers are bidding on Kirk and
the landing party in a slave auction.

"To kill is a breaking of civil and moral laws we've lived by for thousands of years."

Dr. Robert Daystrom, "The Ultimate Computer,"
stardate 4731.3.
Daystrom is trying to reason with
his M-5 computer, which has just
attacked four starships in what it
felt was self-defense.

"We must acknowledge once and for all that the purpose of diplomacy is to prolong a crisis."

Spock, "The Mark of Gideon,"
stardate 5423.4.
Spock realizes he must abide by
Federation rules and honor the wishes
of the people of Gideon by not conducting
a search for Kirk.

"Diplomacy should be a job left to diplomats."

Ambassador Fox, "A Taste of Armageddon,"
stardate 3192.5.
Fox pompously states the above without
any caution to the belligerent events
that have taken place so far.

"In every revolution, there's one man with a vision!"

Kirk, "Mirror, Mirror,"
stardate unknown.
Kirk tries to persuade the Alternate
Spock to reject the Empire's cruel
tactics.

Dr. Richard Daystrom—
THE ULTIMATE COMPUTER

"The customs and history of your race show a unique hatred of captivity. Even when it's pleasant and benevolent, you prefer death. This makes you too violent and dangerous a species for our needs."

The Keeper, "The Menagerie" ("The Cage"),
stardate unknown.
The Talosians have become aware of
all human thought and history.

"Diplomats and bureaucrats may function differently, but they achieve exactly the same results."

Spock, "The Mark of Gideon,"
stardate 5423.4.
Spock replies to Sulu, who is
dissatisfied with the search the people
of Gideon have conducted.

"Philosophic kings have no need of titles."

Parmen the Platonian leader, "Plato's Stepchildren,"
stardate 5784.3.
Parmen tries to illustrate the
liberalism of his utopian society by
telling Kirk he needn't call him "Your
Excellency."

"It's time you learned that freedom is never a gift. It has to be earned."

Kirk, "The Return of the Archons,"
stardate 3157.4.
Kirk wants the people on Beta 3 to
join him in securing their liberty
from Landru.

The Keeper—
THE MENAGERIE

"The problem with the Nazis wasn't simply that their leaders were evil, psychotic men. They were. But the main problem, I think, was the leader principle."
"A man who holds that much power, even with the best intentions, just can't resist the urge to play God."

Kirk and McCoy, "Patterns of Force,"
stardate 2534.7.
Kirk and McCoy discuss the influences
of power.

"You're from the planet Earth. There is no persecution on your planet."
"There was persecution on Earth once; I remember reading about it in my history class."

Lokai of Cheron and Chekov, "Let That
Be Your Last Battlefield,"
stardate 5730.2.
Lokai is trying to make the *Enterprise*
crew understand his prejudice against
Bele of Cheron.

"You'll learn to care for yourselves, with our help. And there's no trick to putting fruit on trees; you might even enjoy it. You'll learn to build for yourselves, think for yourselves, and what you create is yours. That's what we call freedom. You'll like it a lot."

Kirk, "The Apple,"
stardate 3715.6.
Without Vaal, the people of the planet
must build their own society.

"I know this world needs help. That's why some of my generation are kind of crazy and rebels. We wonder if we're going to be alive when we're thirty."

Roberta Lincoln, "Assignment Earth,"
stardate unknown.
Roberta, a product of the rebellious,
protesting and confused 60's generation,
wants to believe Gary Seven's intention
to save the world from a holocaust.

"If change is—inevitable—predictable—beneficial —doesn't logic demand that you be a part of it?"
"One man cannot summon the future."
"But one man can change the present!"

Kirk and the Alternate Spock, "Mirror, Mirror,"
stardate unknown.
The two debate on the Empire's
inevitable doom and the Alternate Spock's
logical course of action.

"If you're speaking of worships of sorts, we represent many beliefs."

McCoy, "Bread and Circuses,"
stardate 4040.7.
McCoy explains to Septimus the Son
Worshipper that they come from a society
which permits freedom of belief and
worship.

CHAPTER TEN

SCIENCE AND TECHNOLOGY

Traditionally, the science in most of science fiction for movies and television went from bad to worse.

Much of that changed with "Star Trek." The series ushered in the era of well-considered science speculation that has kept gaining momentum to this day.

Mr. Spock continually let us see the state of science in the twenty-third century through his comments on galactic life, universal laws, the existence of parallel universes, etc. Throughout the series we are shown technology with plausibility, thanks to outstanding advice from California Technical Institute's Jet Propulsion Laboratory, the Rand Corporation's "Think Tank," and other expert advisors in all areas of science. From the matter/anti-matter engines, to the medical facilities of the ship's sickbay, to the incredible on-board computer,

"Star Trek" uses the very best ideas of today's visionaries to show the world of tomorrow. The quotes in this chapter reflect the intelligence the show has brought to the genre of science fiction, and the intelligence needed for it to become reality.

But because "Star Trek" is first and foremost exciting drama, it enables people who are not science whizzes to be completely engrossed by the program—which in turn enables all of us to more fully understand the lure of "Star Trek."

"Only a fool would stand in the way of progress."

Kirk, "The Ultimate Computer,"
stardate 4725.4.
Kirk is afraid of losing his job
to a machine, but he is also a realist.

"Physical reality is consistent with universal laws. Where the laws do not operate, there is no reality . . . we judge reality by the responses of our senses. Once we are convinced of the reality of a given situation, we abide by its rules."

Spock, "Spectre of the Gun,"
stardate 4385.3.
Spock conjectures that reality does not
apply to the Melkotian planet.

"Physical laws simply cannot be ignored. Existence cannot be without them."

Spock, "Spectre of the Gun,"
stardate 4385.3.
Spock suspects that the Melkotian
planet does not adhere to universal
physical laws.

"We exist in a universe which co-exists with a multitude of others in the same physical space. For certain brief periods of time, an area of their space overlaps an area of ours."

Spock, "The Tholian Web,"
stardate 5693.2.
Spock believes the *Enterprise* has
entered such an area of space.

"Possible existence of a parallel universe has been scientifically conceded."

Spock, "The Alternative Factor,"
stardate 3088.7.
Spock adds credence to Kirk's belief
that the energy source came from another
universe in another dimension, occupying
the same space at the same time.

"We estimate there are millions of planets with intelligent life. We haven't begun to map them."

Kirk, "Metamorphosis,"
stardate 3219.8.
Zefrem Cochrane asks about what it's
like out there in the galaxy.

"I remind you that humans are only a tiny minority in this galaxy."

Spock, "The Apple,"
stardate 3715.6.
Spock is criticizing McCoy's
insistence on applying human standards
to non-human cultures.

"What are the odds in such absolute duplication of life forms in another galaxy?"
"The chances are very much against it."

Kirk and Spock, "By Any Other Name,"
stardate 4657.5.
Kirk and Spock discuss the mathematical
probability of exact duplication of
species.

"Light and warmth! That's necessary to all humanoids."

Kirk, "The Cloud Minders,"
stardate 5818.4.
Kirk admonishes Droxine of Stratos
because her people have denied basic
necessities of life to the Troglytes.

"Without water, we're all just three or four pounds of chemicals."

McCoy, "The Omega Glory,"
stardate unknown.
McCoy has discovered that this is all
that remains of the bodies of the crew
of the *Exeter*.

"The actual theory is that all life forms evolved from the lower levels to the more advanced stages."

Spock, "Let That Be Your Last Battlefield,"
stardate 5730.2.
Bele of Cheron has heard that some of
the people believe they decended
from apes. Spock defines this in a
more scientific manner.

"A mutated, superior man could also be a wonderful thing ... the forerunner of a new and better kind of human being!"

Dr. Elizabeth Dehaver, "Where No Man Has Gone Before,"
stardate 1312.9.
There is growing concern for Mitchell's
new powers, but Elizabeth, beginning to
form feelings for him, defends his new
abilities.

"They're (androids are) perfect. Flawless, mentally and physically. No weaknesses, perfectly disciplined. No vices, no fears, no faults. Just a sense of purpose."

McCoy, "I, Mudd,"
stardate 4513.3.
McCoy is answering Kirk's question
about the psychological readings of
the androids.

"If it is the only survivor of a dead race, to kill it would be a crime against science."

Spock, "The Devil in the Dark,"
stardate 3196.1.
Spock infers it would be advantageous
to capture the creature.

"Instruments register only through things they're designed to register. Space still contains infinite unknowns."

Spock, "The Naked Time,"
stardate 1704.2.
Spock comments on the limitations of
the ship's instruments when confronted
with something unknown.

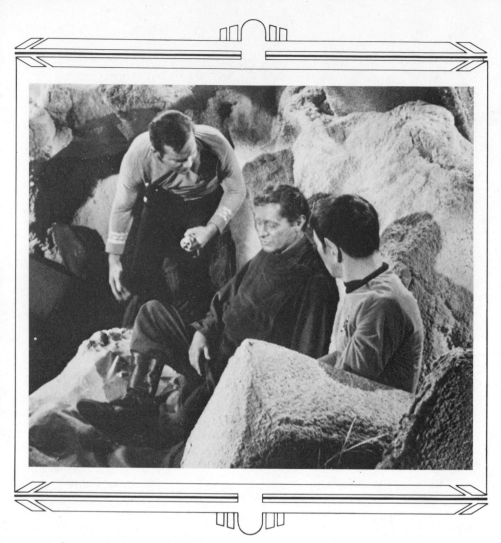

Captain Kirk, Professor Robert Crater, Mr.
Spock—
THE MAN TRAP

"Back in the twentieth century, the H-bomb was the ultimate weapon, their doomsday machine. And we used something like it to destroy another doomsday machine. Probably the first time such a weapon has ever been used for constructive purposes."

Kirk, "The Doomsday Machine,"
stardate 4202.9.
A fusion implosion was created by
overloading the impulse engines of the
crippled *Constellation*, thus destroying
the Doomsday Machine with a peaceful
use of a nuclear device.

"There are certain universal ideas and concepts common to all intelligent life. This device (the universal translator) instantaneously compares the frequency of brain wave patterns, selects those ideas and concepts it recognizes, and then provides the necessary grammar."
"Then it simply translates its findings into English."

Kirk and Spock, "Metamorphosis,"
stardate 3219.8.
Kirk and Spock describe the theory
behind the universal translator to
Zefrem Cochrane.

"Earth history, remember? Like the passenger pigeon, or the buffalo . . . once there were millions of them; prairies black with them. One herd covered three whole states. When they moved—like thunder."

Professor Robert Crater, "The Man Trap,"
stardate 1513.8.
Crater is comparing these extinct
species to the Salt Creature, the
last of its kind.

"As we know, the value of pi *is a transcendental figure without resolution."*

Spock, "Wolf in the Fold,"
stardate 3615.4.
In order to occupy the entity which
has taken over the computer, Spock has
ordered the computer to calculate, to
the last digit, the value of *pi*.

"Less than one ounce of anti-matter here is more powerful than ten thousand cobalt bombs."
"Let's hope it's as powerful as man will ever get."

Ensign Garrovick and Kirk, "Obsession,"
stardate 3620.7.
They are about to lure the creature
to the anti-matter bait which will
annihilate it.

"If I let go of a hammer on a planet having a positive gravity, I need not see it fall to know that it has, in fact, fallen."

Spock, "Court Martial,"
stardate 2948.9.
Spock uses the logic in this statement
to substantiate his knowledge of Kirk's character.

"Crazy way to travel. Spreading a man's molecules all over the universe."

McCoy, "Obsession,"
stardate 3620.7.
McCoy's glib remark when the transporter
malfunctions while Kirk and Ensign
Garrovick are beaming up.

CHAPTER ELEVEN

HUMANITY

"Star Trek" offered a unique opportunity to look at the human race from two perspectives: How humans view humanity and, how aliens view humanity.

But not surprisingly, the people of the twenty-third century are very much like people today. It takes more than a few centuries for human characteristics to change drastically. But change they do.

"Star Trek" sketched a very vivid picture of the growth we will have made by then: prejudice based on a person's appearance or beliefs will be a thing of the past; we will have more understanding and tolerance of our fellow humans, and we will work better together toward common goals; we'll learn to manage nuclear power without destroying ourselves, and we'll have matured enough to hold our killer instincts in check.

Much of the commentary on humanity in the series comes from Captain Kirk, who defends humanity as adeptly as he defends his ship and crew. He may be a hero to his men, but he knows what it is to be a human creature, with all its foibles. Still, he delights in this existence.

Dr. MCoy, too, is familiar with the human animal, both from a professional point of view and on a personal level. He never seems to be at a loss for words to describe our humanity, and by relating these characteristics to the problems of his patients, he is clearly a practitioner of holistic medicine.

The second half of the chapter, the alien point of view, allows us to take an even closer look at ourselves. What we find is that despite our human weaknesses and drawbacks, we emerge with our heads held high, for we are coming of age, this promise of a brighter future for all of humankind being the legacy of "Star Trek."

"All men are brothers."

Kirk, "Bread and Circuses,"
stardate 4040.9.
Kirk says this to Flavius Maximus, to
reassure his beliefs.

" . . . humanity . . . (the) striving of man to achieve greatness through his own resources."

Anton Karidian, "The Conscience of the King,"
stardate 2819.1.
Karidian says that with technology,
mankind has lost the human drive for
greatness. Kirk replies that it still
exists, but man has better tools.

"To be human is also to seek pleasure. To laugh—to dance."

Flint, "Requiem for Methuselah,"
stardate 5843.7.
Flint replies to Kirk's remark on
humans under pressure.

Flint, Captain Kirk—
REQUIEM FOR METHUSELAH

"Being human does have certain advantages—being able to appreciate the beauty of a flower, or a woman."

Kirk, "By Any Other Name,"
stardate 4658.9.
Kirk has convinced Rojan and the other
Kelvans to pursue their own destiny
and future as humans.

" . . . the intellect is not all—but its cultivation must come first, or the individual makes errors—wastes time in unprofitable pursuits."

Flint, "Requiem for Methuselah,"
stardate 5843.7.
Reena Kapec, with the equivalent of
seventeen university degrees, is,
according to Flint, aware that intellect
is not everything.

"My people pride themselves on being the greatest, most successful gamblers in the universe. We compete for everything: power, fame, women. Everything we desire. And it is our nature to win! For proof I offer you our exploration of this galaxy."

Kirk, "The Gamesters of Triskelion,"
stardate unknown.
As a last resort to obtain freedom for
his crew and the Thralls, Kirk challenges
the Providers into a battle. To
emphasize how much of a gambler he is,
he tells the Providers to select weapons
of their own choice.

"Freedom of movement and choice produced the human spirit."

Dr. Brown, "What are Little Girls Made Of?"
stardate 2712.4.
Brown asks Christine if she remembers
this point of Dr. Roger Korby's
teachings.

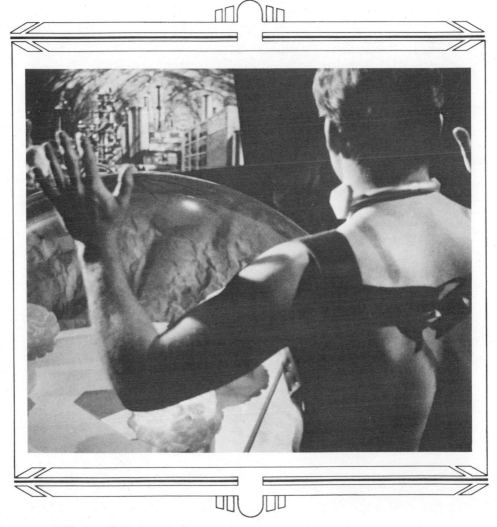

The Providers, Captain Kirk—
THE GAMESTERS OF TRISKELION

"Our species can only survive if we have obstacles to overcome . . . without them to strengthen us, we will weaken and die."

Kirk, "Metamorphosis,"
stardate 3220.3.
The Companion has taken away all the
challenges of life for Zefrem Cochrane,
giving him a sterile immortality.

"We're the same. We share the same history, the same heritage, the same lives. We're tied together beyond any untying. Man or woman, it makes no difference. We're human. We couldn't escape from each other even if we wanted to—that's how you do it, Lieutenant! By remembering who and what you are! A bit of flesh and blood afloat in a universe without end. And the only thing that's truly yours is the rest of humanity. That's where our duty lies!"

Kirk, "Who Mourns For Adonais?"
stardate 3468.1.
Kirk is trying to convince Carolyn Palamas
that her loyalty is to humanity and the
crew, not the god Apollo.

"The semi-conscious mind is a tricky thing. A man never knows just how much is real or how much is imagination."

McCoy, "Obsession,"
stardate 3620.7.
Kirk believes he sensed intelligence
in the creature just before he lost
consciousness.

Lt. Carolyn Palamas, Captain Kirk—
WHO MOURNS FOR ADONAIS?

"It's the custom of my people to help one another when we're in trouble."

Kirk, "The Gamesters of Triskelion,"
stardate 3259.2.
Kirk has demonstrated compassion in
asking to be punished instead of the
Thrall, Shahna, who asks him why he
would do that.

"We've each learned to be delighted with what we are."

Kirk, "The Savage Curtain,"
stardate 5906.4.
Kirk explains his century's lack of
prejudice to Abraham Lincoln.

"Where I come from, size, shape or color makes no difference."

Kirk, "Plato's Stepchildren,"
stardate 5784.3.
Alexander, the Platonian dwarf, wants
to know if there are people his size
where Kirk comes from.

"In our century, we've learned not to fear words."

Uhura, "The Savage Curtain,"
stardate 5906.4.
Abraham Lincoln has called Uhura
"a charming Negress," then wonders if
he has offended her in his choice of
words.

"Now, I don't pretend to tell you how to find happiness and love, when every day is a struggle to survive. But I do insist that you do survive, because the days and the years ahead are worth living for! One day soon, man is going to be able to harness incredible energy—maybe even the atom. Energy that could ultimately hurl men to other worlds in some sort of spaceship. And the men that reach out into space will be able to find ways to feed the hungry millions of the world, and to cure their diseases. They'll be able to find a way to give each man hope and a common future. And those are the days worth living for."

Edith Keeler, "The City on the Edge of Forever,"
stardate unknown.
Edith tells Kirk about her reasons for
being a person who cares and helps others.

"A person's strongest dreams are about what he can't do."

Vina, "The Menagerie" ("The Cage"),
stardate unknown.
Pike has not enjoyed reliving his
past exploits, and Vina begins to realize
what the Keepers must do to entrance him.

"What is man but that lofty spirit—that sense of enterprise."

Kirk, "I, Mudd,"
stardate 4513.3.
Kirk, in trying to confuse the androids,
begins with a true statement about
humankind.

"No wants—no needs? We weren't meant for that. None of us. Man stagnates if he has no ambition, no desire to be more than he is."

Kirk, "This Side of Paradise,"
stardate 3417.5.
Spock, under the influence of the spores,
has just told Kirk that the planet is a
paradise, with no wants or needs.

"Most people are afraid of being alone."

Kirk, "The Mark of Gideon,"
stardate 5423.4.
Odona, from the crowded planet of
Gideon, has stated that all her life
she's dreamed of being alone.

"You know the greatest danger facing us is ourselves, and irrational fear of the unknown. There is no such thing as the unknown. Only things temporarily hidden, temporarily not understood."

Kirk, "The Corbomite Maneuver,"
stardate 1514.0.
Kirk is preparing the crew for the
critical situation the alien has
forced upon them.

"No one knows how he'll act under pressure."

Sulu, "Let That Be Your Last Battlefield,"
stardate 5730.2.
Sulu attempts to console Lokai about
his behavior after the Cheronian
explains his violent actions.

"It is the nature of our species to be free."

Kirk, "Metamorphosis,"
stardate 3219.8.
Kirk is trying to reason with the
Companion for their release.

"When the personality of a human is involved, exact predictions are hazardous."

McCoy, "The Lights of Zetar,"
stardate 5725.6.
Kirk would like to know the long-range
effects of Lt. Romain's near-fatal
encounter with the Zetars.

"Most of us are attracted by beauty and repelled by ugliness—one of the last of our prejudices."

Kirk, "Is There In Truth No Beauty?"
stardate 5630.7.
The Medusan Ambassador is supposed to
be so ugly to look at that it drives
people mad.

"We faced a . . . crisis in our earlier nuclear age. We found the wisdom not to destroy ourselves."

Kirk, "Return to Tomorrow,"
stardate 4768.3.
Kirk tells Sargon that our earlier
nuclear era may have been managed
more wisely than the unleashing of
power which caused a crisis on Sargon's
world.

"We all have our darker side. We need it; it's half of what we are. It's not really ugly, it's human."

McCoy, "The Enemy Within,"
stardate 1673.5.
The divided Kirk doesn't want to take
back his negative self.

"We humans have a streak of barbarism in us—appalling, but there nevertheless."

Kirk, "Space Seed,"
stardate 3141.9.
Kirk appears to be romanticizing
about a ruthless dictator.

"Believe me, there's nothing tougher to overcome (than a sense of purpose), even among humans."

McCoy, "I, Mudd,"
stardate 4513.3.
McCoy answers Kirk's question about
the psychological readings of the
androids.

"In this galaxy, there's a mathematical probability of three million Earth-type planets. And in all of the universe, three million, million galaxies like this. But in all of that, and perhaps more, only one of each of us."

McCoy, "Balance of Terror,"
stardate 1709.9.
Kirk is worried about his responsibilities,
his decisions. McCoy cautions him not
to be so hard on himself.

"Maybe we weren't meant for Paradise. Maybe we were meant to fight our way through. Struggle. Claw our way up, scratch for every inch of the way. Maybe we can't stroll to the music of lutes. We must march to the sound of drums."

Kirk, "This Side of Paradise,"
stardate 3417.7.
Having thrown off the effect of the
spores on Omicron Ceti III, Kirk
comments on man in paradise.

"We are not killers."

Chekov, "Let That Be Your Last Battlefield,"
stardate 5730.6.
Lokai demands that fellow Cheronian,
Bele, be killed.

"To us, killing is murder, even for revenge."

Kirk, "Plato's Stepchildren,"
stardate 5784.3.
Kirk has spared the life of Parmen,
the Platonian leader, even though Kirk
knew Parmen had wanted him dead and the
Enterprise destroyed.

"When a man feels guilty about something—something too terrible to remember—he blots it out of his conscious memory."

McCoy, "Wolf in the Fold,"
stardate 3614.9.
McCoy thinks Scotty may be suffering
from hysterical amnesia.

"We've come a long way in five thousand years."
"But you're still of the same nature."

Kirk and Apollo, "Who Mourns for Adonais?"
stardate 3468.1.
Kirk rebuffs Apollo, who seems to think
humans have remained the same as their
remote ancestors.

"We're a most promising species, Mr. Spock, as
predators go. Did you know that?"
"I frequently have my doubts."
"I don't. Not any more. And maybe in a thousand
years or so, we'll be able to prove it."

Kirk and Spock, "Arena,"
stardate 3046.2.
Kirk and Spock discuss the Metron's
outlook for the human race.

"Mankind has no need for gods. We find the One
quite adequate."

Kirk, "Who Mourns for Adonais?"
stardate 3468.1.
Kirk replies to Apollo's question of
what mankind demands of its gods.

"We think of ourselves as the most powerful beings
in the universe. It's unsettling to discover that we're
wrong."

Kirk, "Errand of Mercy,"
stardate 3201.7.
The discovery of the powers of the
Organians is a shock to Kirk.

"We are all vulnerable, in one way or another."

Kirk, "Is There In Truth No Beauty?"
stardate 5630.7
Dr. Miranda Jones seems vulnerable according to
Dr. McCoy.

"We prefer to help ourselves. We make mistakes, but we're human—and maybe that's the word that best explains us."

Kirk, "I, Mudd,"
stardate 4513.3.
Kirk refuses the android's help.

" 'Let me help.' A hundred years or so from now, I believe, a famous novelist will write a classic using that theme. He'll recommend those three words even over 'I love you.' "

Kirk, "The City on the Edge of Forever,"
stardate unknown.
Kirk is responding to Edith's offer of
help.

"Mankind—ready to kill."
"That's the way it was in 1881."
"I wonder how humanity managed to survive?"
"We overcame our instinct for violence."

Spock and Kirk, "Spectre of the Gun,"
stardate 4385.3.
Spock and Kirk reflect on the emotions
felt by the landing party on the
Melkotian planet.

"Man is not just a biological unit that you can patch together."

McCoy, "The Changeling,"
stardate 3541.9.
McCoy retorts to Nomad that it restored
life to a man, not a machine.

Samuel T. Cogley—
COURT MARTIAL

"I speak of rights! A machine has none; a man must. If you do not grant him that right, you have brought us down to the level of the machine; indeed, you have elevated that machine above us!"

Samuel T. Cogley, "Court Martial,"
stardate 2949.9.
In defending Kirk's word against the
computer, Cogley insists that Kirk has
a right to confront his accuser.

"Your will to survive, your love of life, your passion to know . . . Everything that is truest and best in all species of beings has been revealed by you. Those are the qualities that make a civilization worthy to survive."

Lal the Vian, "The Empath,"
stardate 5121.5.
The Vian tells Kirk what Gem may have
learned from the humans.

"Those pressures are everywhere—in everyone, urging him to what you call 'savagery.' The private hells—the inner needs and mysteries—the beast of instinct. As human beings, that is the way it is. To be human is to be complex. You can't avoid a little ugliness—from within—and from without."

Kirk, "Requiem for Methuselah,"
stardate 5843.7.
Kirk has commented that Flint's
greeting lacked benevolence, to which
Flint has replied that it was the
result of pressures.

"They used to say, if man could fly, he'd have wings. But he did fly; he discovered he had to. Do you wish that the first Apollo mission hadn't reached the moon, or that we hadn't gone on to Mars and then to the nearest star? That's like saying you wish that you still operated with scalpels and sewed your patients up with catgut, like your great, great, great-grandfather used to do . . . Dr. McCoy is right in pointing out the enormous danger potential in any contact with life and intelligence as fantastically advanced as this. But I must point out that the possibilities—the potential for knowledge and advancement is equally great. Risk—risk is our business."

Kirk, "Return to Tomorrow,"
stardate 4768.3.
Kirk allays McCoy's worries about the
danger involved in allowing Sargon and
the others to symbiotically use their
bodies while building humanoid robots.

"Improve a mechanical device and you may double productivity. But improve man, you gain a thousandfold."

Khan Noonian Singh, "Space Seed,"
stardate 3142.8.
The product of selective genetics,
Khan believes himself to be a superior man.

"The time is past. There is no room for gods."

Apollo, "Who Mourns for Adonais?"
stardate 3468.1.
Apollo realizes that he's no longer
needed by mankind.

"The (human) species is capable of much affection."

Deela, the Queen of the Scalosians, "Wink of An Eye,"
stardate 5710.5.
Deela, who has captured Kirk into their
accelerated time, has noted this human
characteristic.

"That's (growing old) been happening to men and women for a long time. I've got the feeling it's one of the pleasanter things about being human, as long as you grow old together."

Zefrem Cochrane, "Metamorphosis,"
stardate 3220.3.
Cochrane will give up his immortality
by staying on the planet.

"You have here an unusual opportunity to appraise the human mind, or to examine, in Earth terms, the roles of good and evil in a man. His negative side, which you call hostility, lust, violence; and his positive side, which Earth people express as compassion, love, tenderness. And what is it that makes one man an exceptional leader? We see here indications that it is his negative side which makes him strong—that his evil side, if you will, properly controlled and disciplined, is vital to his strength. Your negative side removed from you, the power of command begins to elude you."

Spock, "The Enemy Within,"
stardate 1673.1.
Kirk, without his negative half, is
unable to make command decisions.

"Captain, I'm beginning to understand why you Earthmen enjoy gambling. No matter how carefully one computes the odds of success, there is still a certain exhilaration in the risk."

Spock, "Patterns of Force,"
stardate 2534.7.
Spock comments on a pastime enjoyed
by Earthmen, after Kirk's daring plan
of entry into the chancellory works.

"In critical moments men sometimes see exactly what they wish to see."

Spock, "The Tholian Web,"
stardate 5693.2.
While the *Enterprise* is being
held captive by the Tholians, Uhura
believes she has seen the Captain,
although he is presumed dead.

"Humans do have an amazing capacity for believing what they choose—and excluding that which is painful."

Spock, "And The Children Shall Lead,"
stardate 5029.5.
The children show no grief, or even
awareness of their parents' deaths.

"It does often seem that man must fight to live."

Flavius Maximus, "Bread and Circuses,"
stardate 4040.9.
Flavius is having difficulty maintaining
his belief in the brotherhood of man.

"...aloneness. You are so alone. You live out your lives in this shell of flesh, self-contained, separate. How lonely you are; how terribly lonely."

Kollos, the Medusan Ambassador (through Spock), "Is There In Truth No Beauty?" stardate 5630.7.
The Medusan is experiencing human corporeal life for the first time.

"Humans smile with so little provocation."

Spock, "Journey to Babel,"
stardate 3842.3.
Spock's retort to his mother, Amanda. She had assumed he might have taken on more of the human character after so many years among them.

"Curious, how often you humans manage to obtain that which you do not want."

Spock, "Errand of Mercy,"
stardate 3198.4.
Kirk has said they didn't want a war, but they've got one.

"...primitive structure. Insufficient safeguards built in. Breakdown can occur from many causes. Self-maintenance systems of low reliability."

Nomad, "The Changeling,"
stardate 3541.9.
The machine finds the human unit, Scott, an imperfect specimen.

"Where did your race get this ridiculous predilection for resistance? You examine any object; you question everything."

Korob, "Catspaw,"
stardate 3018.2.
Korob, an alien from Pyris VII,
expresses curiosity about Kirk's behavior.

"This thing you call language, though; most remarkable. You depend on it for so very much. But is any one of you really its master?"

Kollos, the Medusan Ambassador (through
Spock), "Is There In Truth No Beauty?"
stardate 5630.7.
The Medusan now experiencing physical
life, reflects doubt that vocal
communication is as important as
we think it is.

"You (humans) are, after all, essentially irrational."

Spock, "Metamorphosis,"
stardate 3220.3.
Zefrem Cochrane tells Spock that he
loves Nancy/The Companion and asks if
that is surprising.

"Oh, how absolutely typical of your species! You don't understand something, so you become fearful."

Trelane, "The Squire of Gothos,"
stardate 2124.5.
Trelane is taking child-like delight in
learning about human instincts.

"These shells in which we have encased ourselves—they have such heightened senses. To feel, to hear, to smell. How do humans manage to exist in these fragile cases?"

Rojan the Kelvan, "By Any Other Name,"
stardate 4657.5.
Rojan and the other Kelvans have taken
on the human form to be more comfortable
and functional on the *Enterprise*.

"There are many aspects of human irrationality I do not yet comprehend. Obsession, for one. The persistent single-minded fixation on one idea."

Spock, "Obsession,"
stardate 3619.6.
Kirk's obsession with the creature
baffles Spock.

"Do you know that you're one of the few predator species that preys even on itself?"

Trelane, "The Squire of Gothos,"
stardate 2124.5.
Trelane is fascinated by the human
species.

"Earthmen like Ramses, Alexander, Ceasar, Napoleon, Hitler, Lee Kuan. Your whole Earth history is made up of men seeking absolute power."

Spock, "Patterns of Force,"
stardate 2534.7.
Spock agrees with the Earth saying
that absolute power corrupts absolutely.

"Man is ultimately superior to any mechanical device."

Kirk, "The Corbomite Maneuver,"
stardate 1514.0.
Kirk replies to McCoy, who has
commented that men are not machines and
cannot continually keep performing at
maximum efficiency.

"We cannot allow any race as greedy and corruptible as yours to have free run of the galaxy."

Norman the android, "I, Mudd,"
stardate 4513.3.
The android believes the galaxy needs to
be protected from mankind.

"Your species is self-destructive."

Norman the android, "I, Mudd,"
stardate 4513.3.
The robot sees flaws in humans and
wants to help by taking over control
of their lives.

"(The Vaalians) have taken their first step (towards achieving true human stature). They've learned to kill."

Spock, "The Apple,"
stardate 3715.6.
Vaal has taught the people of the planet
to kill in an attempt to stop the
interference of Kirk's crew members.

"Earthmen fear to bargain honestly."

Kras the Klingon, "Friday's Child,"
stardate 3497.2.
Kras tells Maab that Kirk and his men
cannot be trusted.

Unidentified Capellan; Kras, the Klingon—
FRIDAY'S CHILD

"You like to think of yourselves as complex creatures, but you're flawed. One gains admittance to your minds through many levels. You have too many to keep track of yourselves. There are unguarded entrances to any human mind."

Sylvia, "Catspaw,"
stardate 3018.2.
Sylvia explains to McCoy, Spock and
Kirk how easily she can control life
forms such as themselves.

"Sparing your helpless enemy who surely would have destroyed you, you demonstrated the advanced trait of mercy, something we hardly expected. We feel that there may be hope for your kind. Therefore you will not be destroyed. It would not be civilized."

Metron, "Arena,"
stardate 3046.2.
The Metron is surprised Kirk has spared
the Gorn and feels there is hope for our
civilization.

"...hesitation...is an hereditary trait of your species, and suddenly faced by the unknown, or imminent danger, a human will invariably experience a split second of indecision. He hesitates."

Spock, "Obsession,"
stardate 3620.7.
Ensign Garrovick doesn't believe that he
did everything he could have in trying
to kill the creature. Spock explains
that his actions were merely human.

"You (humans) find it easier to understand the death of one than the death of a million."

Spock, "The Immunity Syndrome,"
stardate 4307.1.
McCoy has just stated he cannot
comprehend how Spock could feel the
deaths of 400 Vulcans aboard the
starship *Intrepid*.

"You striving, bickering, foolishly brave humans."

Apollo, "Who Mourns for Adonais?"
stardate 3468.1.
He is reminiscing about human nature as
he learned of it when on Earth thousands
of years ago.

"Unhappiness is that state which occurs in the human when wants and desires are not fulfilled."

Spock, "I, Mudd,"
stardate 4513.3.
Kirk has told Alice android #471,
that they are unhappy, and she has
asked for an explanation of the term.

"Humans are very peculiar. I often find them unfathomable, but an interesting psychological study."

Spock, "By Any Other Name,"
stardate 4658.9.
Spock is describing humans to the
Kelvans.

"You are still half-savage—but there is hope."

Metron, "Arena,"
stardate 3046.2.
Kirk has spared the life of the Gorn,
and by showing this mercy, the highly
advanced Metrons feel that the human
race shows promise.

The Metron—
ARENA

ODDS AND ENDS

"A lie is a very poor way to say hello."

Edith Keeler, "The City on the Edge of Forever,"
stardate unknown.
When Edith discovers Kirk and Spock in
the basement of the mission house and
asks what they are doing there, they
reply that they were escaping the cold,
when they were actually hiding from the
police.

"Hours can be centuries."

Vanna the Troglyte, "The Cloud Minders,"
stardate 5819.0.
Kirk has promised to return in a short
time, but Vanna does not believe he
will return to help her people.

"Be pleasant no matter how much it hurts."

Kirk, "Elaan of Troyius,"
stardate 4372.5.
Kirk cautions Scott about his attitude
toward the diplomatic guests aboard
ship who have taken an interest in the
engineering room equipment.

"Parents like stupid things."

Don, one of the Starnes Expedition
children, "And The Children Shall Lead,"
stardate 5029.5.
Don expresses a thought that most
children, at one time or another, think
about their parents.

*"I think children have an instinctive need for adults;
they want to be told right and wrong."*

Kirk, "Miri,"
stardate 2713.6.
Kirk comments on why Miri, one of the
300-year-old children, wants to stay
with Kirk and company. Actually she has
fallen in love with Kirk.

"A room should reflect its occupant."

Kirk, "Wink of An Eye,"
stardate 5710.5.
Deela, the Queen of the Scalosians, has
remarked that Kirk's quarters are quite
like him—austere, efficient and
handsome.

*"A library serves no purpose unless someone is
using it."*

Atoz of Sarpeidon, "All Our Yesterdays,"
stardate 5943.7.
Mr. Atoz is the librarian on Sarpeidon
and has offered his services to the
Enterprise landing party.

"Sailor's luck, Mr. Spock. Or as one of Finagle's Laws puts it: 'Any home port the ship makes will be somebody else's, not mine!'"

Kirk, "Amok Time,"
stardate 3372.7.
Kirk's light-hearted remark to a somber
Spock, concerning Starfleet's command
altering their flight plan.

"In the long history of medicine, no doctor has ever caught the first few minutes of play."

McCoy, "The Conscience of the King,"
stardate 2819.8.
The special performance of *Hamlet* is
about to begin, and McCoy is working in
sickbay.

"We're immortal, we gods. The Earth changed. Your fathers changed. They turned away, until we were only memories. A god cannot survive as a memory. We need love, admiration, worship, as you need food."

Apollo, "Who Mourns for Adonais?"
stardate 3468.1.
Lt. Carolyn Palamas receives a first-
hand lesson in ancient mythology from
Apollo.

"Nobody helps nobody but himself!"

Bela Oxmyx, "A Piece of the Action,"
stardate unknown.
Bela cannot understand Spock and McCoy's
offer to help.

"Make the most of an uncertain future. Enjoy yourself today. Tomorrow—may never come at all."

Trelane, "The Squire of Gothos,"
stardate 2125.7.
Kirk is anxious to get back to the
Enterprise and away from this maniac.

"It isn't a bad life to have everyone in the universe at your beck and call, and you win all the arguments."

Kirk, "The Man Trap,"
stardate 1513.8.
The Salt Vampire, a proven killer, can
become anything Professor Crater
desires, and Kirk sarcastically chastises
him for protecting it.

"I don't trust men who smile too much."

Commander Kor, "Errand of Mercy,"
stardate 3201.7.
The Klingon Commander Kor has established
himself as military dictator of Organia, apparently
a passive society of perpetually smiling
beings.

"The cat is the most ruthless, most terrifying of animals. As far back as the sabertooth tiger . . ."

Spock, "Catspaw,"
stardate 3018.2.
Sylvia, in order to terrify, has
transformed herself into a cat.

"Sometimes pain can drive a man harder than pleasure."

Kirk, "The Alternative Factor,"
stardate 3088.7.
McCoy has told Kirk that Lazurus is
in a lot of pain.

"The most cooperative man in this world is a dead man."

Bela Oxmyx, "A Piece of the Action,"
stardate unknown.
Bela expresses to Spock his personal philosophy
regarding unity and cooperation.

"The trigger has been pulled. We've got to get there before the hammer falls."

Kirk, "Errand of Mercy,"
stardate 3198.4.
War is imminent, and Kirk must prevent
the Klingons from using Organia as a
base. However, convincing the Organians
of the impending war will be time consuming
and difficult.

"Hot as Vulcan."

McCoy, "Amok Time,"
stardate 3372.7.
Vulcan, a planet whose air is thin, hot
and dry, averages about 140 degrees during
the day. McCoy now understands what
the phrase means.

"May the Great Bird of the galaxy bless your planet."

Sulu, "The Man Trap,"
stardate 1513.4.
Yeoman Rand has brought Sulu some
food, while he tends to the botanical lab.

"Live long and prosper."

—Spock of Vulcan

APPENDIX

We would like to express our personal thanks to all of the "Star Trek" writers whose stories made up the original television series. It was their inspiring words and thoughts which enabled us to conceive this book.

Our appreciation also to Allen Asherman for making available his extensive collection of "Star Trek" photographs, and Bjo Trimble, for providing the dialogue continuity scripts from which we compiled our material.

"Star Trek" had many things to say, as evidenced in the pages of this book. Quotes were obtained from all but two of the original seventy-nine one-hour episodes. "Tomorrow is Yesterday" and "Whom Gods Destroy" were the exceptions. These were entertaining and interesting stories, but we did not find there was anything relevant to quote.

The following pages provide an alphabetical listing of all the episodes from which quotes were taken. The number, or numbers, next to each title refer to the page, or pages, in the book where you can locate the particular episode.

One final thought: a special thanks to Gene Roddenberry. He has shared his optimistic and enthusiastic view of the future with all of us, and made us believe that space is truly the final frontier, and we will indeed go where no man has gone before!

"All Our Yesterdays" 50, 152
By Jean Lissette Aroeste